PRAISE FOR *BLAC*

"Young's revealing sentences scu
nna Valley that is both tender and terrifying. "

> —TAYLOR BRORBY, author of *Boys and Oil:*
> *Growing Up Gay in a Fractured Land*

"Catherine Young paints a lovely and dreamlike poem-portrait of her childhood in a Pennsylvania coal town. *Black Diamonds* beautifully captures a transformative moment in American history and is a skillfully written and remarkable ode to Place."

> —JONATHAN P. THOMPSON, author of
> *Sagebrush Empire: How a Remote Utah County*
> *Became The Battlefront of American Public Lands*

"Young is a poet of superb gifts that inform her prose at every turn. *Black Diamonds* is a book to treasure that is full of stories that are rich in memory and landscape."

—JAY PARINI, author of *Borges and Me: An Encounter*

"With Young's remarkable gift for description, she depicts the cost of the Pennsylvania coal boom to the land and the families who mined it with a loving honesty and a lyricism that will honor the Lackawanna Valley and its people for a long time to come."

> —NATALIE S. HARNETT, author of *The Hollow*
> *Ground*, winner of the Appalachian Book of theYear
> Award and the John Gardner Book Award

"*Black Diamonds* tells a compelling story of the complicated love of place particular to coal communities. Young brings a refreshing new voice to our grasp of geographical kinship. This much-needed memoir offers a uniquely empathetic critique of extractive communities. I look forward to placing it on my shelf next to Terry Tempest Williams' *Refuge*."

—JOHN HAUSDOERFFER, co-author and co-editor of
What Kind of Ancestor Do You Want to Be?

"A fascinating, imperative recollection of her early years growing up in a fossil fuel economy, *Black Diamonds* is a tale told only as Catherine Young could tell it. It's beautifully written with rich detail and warmth, from a place of memory, love and escape. Reading this, I now have an intimacy with the Lackawanna Valley and its industry I could not have expected and for that I am grateful."

—SIMMONS BUNTIN, Editor-in-Chief, Terrain.org,
author of *Unsprawl: Remixing Spaces as Places*

"An breathtaking memoir. Young's voice is electrifying."

—ALEXIS POWELL, The King's English Bookshop

"Together with George Inness's famous *The Lackawanna Valley* painting, Young vividly depicts the anthracite coal town of her childhood. As she recounts life in coal country in the 1960s, she deftly weaves together threads of hardship and comfort, grief and acceptance, and change and stagnation. With poetic and evocative prose, Young's *Black Diamonds* reveals how coal—like its black dust—is inescapable."

—ARYN G. N. SCHRINER, University of Maryland

BLACK DIAMONDS

BLACK DIAMONDS

A Childhood Colored by Coal

CATHERINE YOUNG

TORREY HOUSE PRESS

Salt Lake City • Torrey

"Coal Year" was first published in *Kestrel*, Issue 37: Spring 2017.
A version of "A Cup of Tea" was first published in *Punctuate: A
Nonfiction Magazine*, March 2017.

First Torrey House Press Edition, September 2023

Published by Torrey House Press
Salt Lake City, Utah
www.torreyhouse.org

International Standard Book Number: 978-1-948814-83-6
E-book ISBN: 978-1-948814-84-3
Library of Congress Control Number: 2022951344

Cover art: *The Lackawanna Valley*, c 1856, George Inness, National
Gallery of Art | Cover photo: The Lackawanna Valley, c. 1959, Library
of Congress.
Cover design by Kathleen Metcalf
Interior design by Rachel Buck-Cockayne
Distributed to the trade by Consortium Book Sales and Distribution

Torrey House Press offices in Salt Lake City sit on the homelands of
Ute, Goshute, Shoshone, and Paiute nations. Offices in Torrey are on
the homelands of Southern Paiute, Ute, and Navajo nations.

With advice from Catherine Young, this book was set in 12 pt Times
New Roman font to help improve accesibility for the visually impaired.

For Barry, Carmella, and Fuzzy
Our stories were wedded and woven like paired iron rails
threaded along each ravine and riverway.

Contents

The Lackawanna Valley, c. 1856, George Inness,
National Gallery of Art.

The Valley

We zoom along an interstate highway across Pennsylvania's thickly forested mountains. The road, like all interstates, is broad and straight, ignoring all the twists and turns, the deep, sinuous curves and valleys of this landscape. Forests blur. All I can see are the tilted and layered gray shales of these mountain road cuts.

From my back-seat view, the driver is handsome, his wife, petite and smiling. Son and daughter on the back seat beside me are young and curious, not at all uncomfortable with a stranger in their midst. I have just met the family at a gathering. They've offered to give me a ride back to the town where I am staying with friends—a small town on a mountain above the Lackawanna Valley. In this short ride, I've learned they have recently relocated from a neighboring state. His job: manager. His wife: well-educated, a professional giving time to her children and family.

And now my turn. "So you're from the Midwest…" the mother says over her shoulder. "Visiting?"

"Yes. My friend's in your town." I leave it at that. I look out the window at the familiar gray shales. So dark. Not at all like the golden shales in the Mississippi River Valley where I now live. I don't want to tell them this is where I am from. It was all too hard and sad growing up here in Eastern Pennsylvania's anthracite coal country, and I wanted to believe I was beyond this place…a land tainted by coal dust and sulfur smoke, an ashen, abandoned land of desperate people in poverty with nowhere to go. A place looked down upon. To change the subject, I ask the couple how they like their town, the pretty one above the Lackawanna Valley.

"It's a lovely town. A really nice place for raising kids."

"Big trees along the streets. Small town neighborhood feeling."

I nod. "It is a sweet place." And then the small talk takes a turn I'm unprepared for.

"People are great here," the man says, meaning the people in their small town. "But the *Valley People*!" The contempt in his voice overwhelms me. *Valley People.* For a moment, the breath is knocked out of me. "You mean the people living in the Lackawanna Valley?" I ask.

"Yeah. Those people are so backward. You should see how they dress—like something out of the 1940s."

The wife picks up the story. "Have you seen their houses? They probably haven't painted them since then either. Everything is so dirty!"

"And that downtown Scranton." The man shakes his head. "They let it burn and didn't even take down the structures. Every other building is empty or boarded up!"

Images from my childhood rise before me: coal trains, relief lines, toothless women wearing babushkas. I hear the rattling of coal on ramps, coal burning in basements. The smell of burning and stinking sulfur everywhere…

"...so, there's no real shopping area there!" the wife adds, holding up her hands. "There's no development. They don't do anything!"

The man shakes his head. "So ignorant. People just sit on their porches—staring. It's eerie...as if no one ever comes down their street!"

My face burns as my internal dialogue takes off. Yes, that's true. When you don't have a car and city buses don't run like they used to, all you can do is sit on your porch and stare. And porches—well, that's the way you spend your time in summer. Or at least, we did.

The wife fires one more volley. "You can't find a decent café anywhere. Can you *imagine*?"

Here in the 1980s? Yes, I can imagine. No latté. My heart races. Those *Valley People*. So ignorant. As the miles along the interstate click past, the words smolder in me. I've done well crossing over into another life. Midwestern, middle class, professional. Not from clothes, speech, or demeanor can they guess this valley as my place of origin. I nod to myself. And it's as I suspected all along growing up: there are "rich people" who live above the valley who can come and go, do as they please, and there are the people in the valley (mostly widows when I was growing up) who are just stuck. I'm sure the people in the pretty small town didn't lose their skin to poisonous air as many of us in the valley did.

The anger from my childhood ignites. I want to shout: Who says we're not good enough? Who says we're backward? What's wrong with wearing clothes from the 1940s if they're still good? Into the 1970s old women still wore

clothing styles from the nineteenth century or the old country because they kept their traditions—or couldn't afford to
change. I need to say something to this couple, but I'm
unsure how to begin.

What happens next must be divine intervention. We
pass the sign for the Davis Street exit, and the man asks
me, "So, how did you come to have connections in this
area—so far from your home?"

We pass through a road cut, and I see a cleft in the
mountain ridge on the right side that shows a brook. I
pause and take a breath. "I grew up here," I reply.

"Oh?"

"Yes. I grew up in *The Valley*. I'm a *Valley Person*."
The couple is silent. "You see this hollow we're coming
to…it's a little neighborhood on the edge of Scranton. It's
where I grew up. This was my neighborhood."

As we cross the interstate highway bridge, I look over
at the steep hillside on the left covered with dingy clapboard houses. Down beneath this bridge, hidden from
view of this highway, is my dad's grave and those of all
his relatives. I want to say to the couple: I can name each
tree over there. I know every tree along those tree-named
streets, every sidewalk and every crack. Mama and I
walked along railroad tracks that used to run right there,
beside the highway—tracks that were used for a century.
We picked berries here, between the rocks and the tracks
before this interstate was built. My mama and I walked the
whole hollow on down the mile to the valley bottom, to
church, to downtown and back again. When I was growing
up here, everything was black with coal—coal along all
the many rail lines leading away from the city, along the

river, along our streets—and our city was large and tall and proud.

And it's all gone now. I want to say all this to the family, to have them see what I knew: houses filled with hard-working people, yards filled with gardens and coops, the creek, the cemetery, the hospitals full of men gasping for breath, everywhere trains and coal. But…how can they see it? Interstates have a duty to move people through quickly. The landscape shifts before I can say a word. We ride on in uncomfortable silence, passing over my neighborhood with its dilapidated coal-fueled houses; we ride in a car on pavement that took away part of my neighborhood and forever after gave us roaring cars and trucks day and night as if we didn't matter at all.

Even before 1986, the time of that car ride, the Lackawanna Valley was a place plagued by no jobs and no hope. The ugliness of the anthracite mining towns was legendary. Culm dumps, the piles of waste coal four stories tall, burning, filling the air with acrid smoke. Smoke rising in the streets from fires in the mines beneath them. Orange waters. Houses covered in soot. Houses with peeling paint resulting from the sulfuric acid-drenched air—the acid rain. Empty downtown buildings. Buildings and streets and yards collapsing into mines. In Scranton, a county courthouse square surrounded by homeless men living on benches. The complete collapse of the anthracite economy in my childhood in the 1960s had left the Lackawanna Valley in the condition the couple saw it, and I, trying to make my way in the world, needed to wash my hands of the black dust and rusty stains of coal.

And yet, for a few years following that car ride, I was indignant. I ranted to my close friends. *Who* was ignorant? How could educated people of my generation not know about the Lackawanna Valley and its history? It was the birthplace of the industrial revolution in North America, the place where fuel came from: coal to make steel for rails and run the railroads, coal to power the factories and generate electricity all across the United States. Coal to provide gas for cooking. Coal to heat homes all over America.

But by the 1980s, the glory days of black diamonds and steel rails were gone. Though black veins of anthracite still lay in the roots of those mountains, coal was no longer mined there to fuel a nation, or heat homes, or boil a kettle of water for tea. It was no longer possible to see collieries, or mile-long strings of anthracite-filled coal cars, or culm dumps. In the 1960s and 70s, the mines were shut down, then flushed with culm and water to put the raging minefires out. The railroads that lined our lives were consolidated and abandoned: first the passenger trains, then freight, and then stations, tracks, signals, rails, and men. The tie spikes stamped with the years of their fabrication poked up from the wooden ties as they rotted, and when the spikes were pilfered, no one did the gandydance of the tracklayers to put it all back together again.

—

In 1991, five years after the ride on the interstate with that family, I returned to the Lackawanna Valley—this time with my husband for what became my last trip there. My high school, the library, the philharmonic hall, and department stores were closed down. I had come to pick up the remains of my belongings: Grandma's crumbling cardboard satchel of family photos, dozens of doilies and dresser scarves crocheted and embroidered by many old aunties' hands. And my Honeybun.

Honeybun was my first friend. My beloved companion. My family might have called him a stuffed rabbit. A toy. Something for me to hold in my crib.

But Honeybun was much more than that. My gray rabbit was very real to me. His shiny pink eyes winked at me, and he cuddled up in my arms at night. Honeybun was my true baby friend.

I brought Honeybun home with me on our flight back to the Midwest. He rode in the overhead luggage, close-padded in doilies, dresser scarves, and old photos.

At home, I sorted and cleaned my reclaimed treasures. I dusted photos of people standing in yards—people from another century—my people—some of whom I had never gotten to meet. Yet I knew their names and the important dates of their lives from years of asking Grandma, my dad's mom, in her kitchen, and Auntie and Little Grandma, my mother's family, in their parlor. All the photographs were of people staring directly into the camera, claiming a moment in their lives for posterity—relatives who had crossed an ocean and posed in their best clothes. Grandparents in high-top shoes recording a day at the mountain lake. Children I knew only as middle-aged or elderly relatives holding a batch of puppies long gone. I studied the faces in the photographs the way I was taught to—searching for features that I carry—and I tried to figure out how much happiness they had. What would they think of me? Could any of them have imagined I would move to another part of the country a thousand miles away from where they had settled? Beyond the mountains might as well have been the moon. Could they have dreamed of how women's lives would change in a century?

I found a dark cloth in which to wrap the photos, and I put them away.

I took each lacy doily and washed it by hand in a basin much the way Mama would have. The pungent smell of sulfur and old wood placed me in Grandma's house, Mama's attic, the kitchens, the basements full of coal ash. The odors arose in waves each time I squeezed a cloth in my hands, and with each wave I felt such sadness for the loss of the old women from both sides of the family. All these pieces of lace had been packed away for special times—for gifts at weddings. Why is it I never before saw how beautiful the handwork was? So many pieces of lace, enough to cover every dresser in a home several times over. Enough to allow Mama to rotate the doilies every season. Round doilies, star-shaped doilies, large enough to cover a table, every pattern imaginable. So many hours of women's hands spiraling with a metal hook. What thoughts did they have as they transformed delicate cotton thread into intricate webs of beauty? I saw Mama in her flowered full-skirted dress receiving these beautiful gifts, pointing to each creator, and saying, "Look at this. Look how she can crochet! Maybe she'll teach you someday!"

After many days of slow work, I got all the cloths washed, hung to dry, and put away.

Lastly, I looked at Honeybun. How to help him?

Patches of fur were gone; a metal button eye was loose.

His little bunny tail was missing. He was lumpy. The satin pink of his inner ears was frayed to threads.

Carefully, I cut off the satin. I opened the stitches to remove the lumpy cotton stuffing. I took the pelt of my beloved gray bunny to the sink and began to wash. As his face submerged, I was stunned by what I saw. The water turned milky gray, and my Honeybun, my gray baby friend, wasn't really gray. His fur was white, and all the years of coal dust melted away. I burst into tears. Honeybun was white.

I cleaned and dried his fur, patched his ears with pink cloth. I reattached the loose eye button. I filled him with wool and sewed him back up, and I made a new tail for him. Honeybun was all back together, but he left an opening in me.

Behind him I saw my parents in their bedroom, the radiator chugging and hissing. My parents leaning over me, allaying my fears about the radiator, putting Honeybun in my arms, reassuring me: "You'll be okay, honey. The radiator is there to keep us warm. You hold on to Honeybun. He'll keep you safe in the dark." I heard the trains thrumming up out of the Lackawanna Valley. I saw the light outside the window—sparkling snow under the streetlamp, glittering diamonds falling from a low sky. I smelled coal and ash.

I heard the fears in my parents' voices with each mine closure, each breaker becoming empty, with each downtown building mysteriously burned. "The trains are going to stop running…We might lose passenger service. How can we have a city without the trains?"

My dad's voice came echoing from my childhood: "This place will be a ghost town—just highways and banks."

I saw it all—mountains of ash, the culm dumps covered in blue flames, shadowy trains, long, long strings of coal cars going away full and coming home empty. Bridges of black iron crossing over and under us everywhere. Lights in the valley at night. Rumbling. Smoke.

I realized that I had a gallery of paintings that had remained locked in the vault of my heart. I wanted to open the doors and bring them out into the light to be seen, these images of a childhood colored by coal.

THE *WORLD BOOK* SPEAKS

World Book Encyclopedia 1957, volume 15, S page 7287-7288:

Scranton

SCRANTON, Pa. (Population 125,536), is the largest city in the Pennsylvania anthracite coal region, which is the greatest coal region of its kind in the world. The Scranton region ranks high in the manufacture of silk. Scranton has changed from a mining and manufacturing city. It is now a major textile, household appliance, and shoe-manufacturing center. The city is the fourth largest in population in the state. **It was named for the Scranton family, which founded in iron works here in 1840.**

Scranton lies in northeastern Pennsylvania, 134 miles from New York City and 18 miles northeast of Wilkes-Barre. The city is **set in a deep valley that is closely bordered by ridges of the Allegheny Mountains.**

The coal beds here are wider and of greater thickness than in most places, and so near the surface that some cave-ins have occurred in the city.

The People. Work in the coal mines brought people of several European nationalities to the Scranton region at different times. The first settlers were the Welsh, the Germans, and the Irish. Later came the Poles, Czechs, Italians, and Lithuanians. Today, however, the city does not have an unusually large population of foreign-born persons.

Cultural Life. Scranton is the home of the International Correspondence Schools, the largest of their kind in the world. Also located here are the University of Scranton, Marywood College (for girls), Scranton-Lackawanna College (business training), and the Scranton Conservatory of Music.

Industry and Trade. Scranton has a large wholesale and retail trade. Besides coal, Scranton produces lace, heating and air-conditioning equipment, plastic products, mining and textile machinery, grates, stokers, stoves, paints and varnishes, condensers, photograph records, paper boxes, white lead, and clothing.

History. The first settlers came to this region in the 1780s. As late as 1849 there were only five houses in the community. In that year, however, Scranton began to grow. **The first railroad entered Scranton in 1851.** It became a borough in 1853 and a city in 1866.   R.O.H.

I. The Painting: Sunset View

Growing up in Pennsylvania's Lackawanna Valley, I was in love with a landscape painting.

George Inness's *The Lackawanna Valley* sang in my heart. Pastel greens and blues, lavender, gold, and rose. A little black steam locomotive, a boy, a pasture, blue mountains, and a fledgling city below them. My city: Scranton, Pennsylvania, as it was in the 1850s, one hundred years before I was born.

Here and there I would get flashes of Inness's painting, in textbooks or library books. Once, I believe, I even saw it in the local museum. I was haunted by Inness's depiction of my home place. Except for the mountains on a rare clear day, nothing else in my childhood looked like that painting.

In the center of a sweeping scene of an Appalachian mountain landscape, a steam locomotive, with funnel smokestack and pointed cowcatcher, is rounding a curve, and crossing a wooden bridge to begin its long journey up and out of the valley. Its cumulus plume of steam stretches over cab and tender and fades out over a string of coal cars that follow.

In the left foreground, a graceful tree, elm-like, arches over the scene: tall, vase-shaped, and classical in elegance.

Beside the tree a red-vested, straw-hatted boy reclines on the ground, leaning on his elbow. He faces the approaching locomotive with its cars in tow. Around him, cut close to the ground, evenly spaced tree stumps expose a grassy pasture where farther away, a brown cow lies.

The train has crossed through a verdant band—trees that indicate a river hidden from view—and it has left behind a huge brick roundhouse and a broad avenue paralleling the tracks. Farther back in the scene, houses, brick warehouses, and a church spire fade into the mist. And yet farther back, in the center of the painting almost lost from sight, two faint plumes of smoke rise against the background of forested mountains.

The softly rounded Endless Mountains rise above rails and buildings. A rosy glow meets the misty blue edges and fades to a pale expanse at the top of the sky.

All is neatly laid out in the Inness painting: the land and water, the mountains and sky, the trees and the boy, the locomotive, the industrial revolution coming through. But the painting is also composed of iron and coal. Of greed. Of pigment. Of a viewpoint.

All these parts comprise the scene and begin the story of how the famed Lackawanna Valley's industry began, grew, and powered a nation; how it was the engine of the industrial revolution in America; how, over time, it decayed and was left desolate. It all comes back to George Inness's train on the bridge—a bridge from one era to another. The locomotive in the painting crosses into a whole new world of speed and power through iron and coal.

—

The gallery of paintings in my heart begins with this most famous Inness painting, *The Lackawanna Valley,* for it shaped my childhood perceptions of my own landscape and its hues. Inness's canvas is intricately interwoven into my memory—it is my sight line of the valley.

The sweep of the landscape comes back to me with the colors of distance: the unmistakable misty blue of those mountains, rounded and humped like the backs of slow, great beasts gone into an enchanted sleep. The rosy glow Inness painted above his mountain scene is so familiar. Standing at the top of my hill, looking west over the Lackawanna Valley at sunset, that rosy view took my breath away.

Rose and blue: calming colors—the paired colors of a living heart.

Color and memory paint my landscape story. But both color perception and memory are unique to each person. And color—like memory—transforms over time. It can fade, or glow brighter like coals given fresh air. It can shine with iridescence, fluoresce in the darkness under another kind of light.

When I was a child, George Inness gave me a magic window into the world before my time. I wanted to be the boy in the Inness painting. I wanted to ride his shoulder to witness the first locomotives cutting through the landscape—and more, I wanted to see the land before the time of coal's extraction. I wanted to stand with George Inness and his blank canvas.

I always wondered where Inness had stood when he set his vision of the Lackawanna Valley in pigments and oils. Was it in my neighborhood, facing west across the Lackawanna Valley at sunset—perhaps just a little farther downslope into the valley and closer to the DL&W, the Delaware, Lackawanna & Western railroad station? I wondered if I could find the hidden outlines of Inness's vision at sunset. Even as a girl looking down into the Lackawanna Valley at twilight, I sought beauty. I imagine that girl this way:

She climbs up the steep street she lives on, away from her little hollow, and stands atop her hill at dusk, next to the tall brick hospital that overlooks the broad, deep, smoke-filled valley. Behind her, the hollow fills with shadows. Before her, from the top of the sky to the rim of the western mountains, colors drop in layers of light, golden-white to rose to cornflower blue. Below the mountain edges, smoke layers the valley down to the very bottom where smoking culm dumps, the piles of burning waste coal, line a river so hidden by rails, bridges, and buildings that no one can see the water.

This painting is in motion. The girl reaches her arms out to the setting sun, for she believes she is directing it. The girl sweeps her arms across her small arc of sky, and the sun sets. She's deeply satisfied watching the colors shift. The lightness of sky disappears, the smoke is no longer visible. Now, just now, at this moment of transition, the valley is so beautiful. And though the girl stands beside a steeply tilting asphalt road lined with triangular roofed houses all around her, the buildings dropping down the steep mile to the river seem for a moment to vanish into mist. The blue of the West Mountain edge and the rose of the twilight lift the girl's heart, suspend her in the moment, in the landscape, in the joy of a discovered wildness.

The balance tips. The light shifts again. All fades to blue, deeper blue, to black. The valley fills with lights. Rumbles and rattles echo into the night: slamming boxcars, slamming couplers, grinding locomotives, shrieking metal wheels. Star-like white lights appear along trails and roads. Dim yellow lights shine from houses stacked against one another on a dark, folded landscape carpet.

Another light begins to glow. Mysterious cobalt flames appear ghostlike up and down the conical culm mountains of coal waste mounded along the valley floor. Flickering, disappearing, reappearing, fading, the flames flow like a blue aurora borealis come to earth. The girl cannot see the blue flames from this place high above the valley bottom, but she knows they're there. From her father's car, she has seen the flames when they've driven past the sinister and horrible breaker buildings and the enormous culm dumps. The blue flames are demons that show themselves only at night, dancing across the burning culm.

It's time to go. The girl turns away from the great valley and faces the miniature valley of her hollow. She looks across to East Mountain curving up before her. Rimming the mountain across the ravine from where she stands, dark shapes glide and shriek. One small light leads the way, bumping the shadows through the woods, moving from right to left. One small square window glides by, where a man sits guiding the locomotive. To the left of the scene, red lights flash left and right, left and right, and bells sound with the railroad crossing guards' descent. First the loco-motive, and then the trucks and wheels of gondola cars pass, silhouetted by the headlights of one beetle-shaped automobile waiting on the other side of the tracks.

The girl is frozen by the motion of this train gliding on the dark mountainside across from her. There is no time-table for this train line moving coal from one hollow to another. The trains come and go at any time on these rails, slicing daylight or darkness. Though she would command a sunset, the girl stands silently across the ravine watching this train pass. Still holding the colors of sunset inside her, the girl lets go the task of counting the cars this time. She waits until the little hat-shaped silhouette of the caboose roof passes through the beetle-car's headlights, and begins her descent. The car at the crossing speeds away, and the girl walks back down the street into the hollow below the mountain, to her house.

Dark and Light

Even before my memory of Honeybun, my most powerful memory of Dad with Mama and me is so very early, my parents told me I couldn't possibly have remembered. Yet when I recounted details, they relented.

In the beginning is the darkness—a warmth bound by coarse cotton sheets and their bodies surrounding me, Mama's and Dad's. I am frightened by the darkness and cry out.

"What's wrong, baby?" my mama asks softly. "Did you slip too far under the sheets?" They reach for me, pull me up from under the covers, and beach me on the pillows. Their faces touch mine in the dark room and we sleep.

♦ ♦ ♦

When I think of Mama, I feel her hand holding mine, for we were always walking to my dad's mom's house, to church, to downtown, to the museum and park, to the hospital, to the cemetery. She could only walk to where she wanted to go. She did not drive a car. She could take a bus to visit her family in the adjacent small town, but she couldn't do it without me in tow. I was her constant companion. Often, I was an anchor, dragging Mama to slow her steps, trudging back home from church or downtown, climbing up the impossibly steep streets ascending from the valley. In nearly all the scenes of my childhood, she is ever-present, like a Madonna in a church, and just as beautiful in her plainness.

Mama was always there. And Dad was not.

♦ ♦ ♦

If I think of Dad, I cannot remember as many scenes with him in them. I didn't see him that much—or that's how it felt. He was a city firefighter, and he worked a strange rotating schedule, sleeping away from home for days. His work schedule was grueling—four days of twelve-hour shifts, four nights of twelve-hour shifts, four days off— and then the schedule began again, always shifting, so that Dad slept at odd times. At home, he sat at the table with coffee and a cigarette—or sleeping. He was mostly sleeping. Sometimes he was called out from sleep at home to a general alarm fire.

My memories of Dad come to me in flashes of short, sweet scenes. I remember seeing him at the Fire Headquarters dressed in the gray uniform work shirt, greeting Mama and me on a visit downtown. He rises from the card table in the back room and gives me a quick hug. Everything smells sharply of the kerosene used to clean the trucks. He shows me the fire pole and puts me on a truck for only a few seconds, his arms encircling me in case the alarm goes off—which it could at any second of the day. The fleeting moments at the fire station feel like joyous family reunions.

I am sitting on Dad's lap as he guides our old car through the hollow the few short blocks to his mother's house. He is on his way to bring her groceries, check on her, feed her furnace with shovelfuls of Chestnut coal, and take out ashes. Grandma is old and infirm and doesn't leave home at all. Nor can she do the tasks that living with coal requires.

Dad places my hands on the wheel and has me steer as he drives the car through the hollow, ever so slowly. "Don't tell Mama," he whispers in my ear.

A thunderstorm begins to rumble up our hollow. Dad races with me out to the back porch, swinging me up onto the discarded kitchen table to give me a view of the storm heading our way. Arms wrapped around my shoulders, Dad shouts with each flash of lightning, and together we cheer and clap for each thundering boom as if we are in the best stadium in the world.

Dad is in the hospital again, with asthma, hemorrhaging so bad that he remains for days within an oxygen tent over the bed. He has the same health problems that afflict so many men in the valley, illnesses from a combination of breathing smoke-filled air and a ubiquitous addiction to cigarettes—but he has collapsed fighting a fire. The Catholic hospital just up the street becomes a gathering place for Dad's part of the family.

——————————— ♦ ♦ ♦ ———————————

There is another memory from when I was quite small. I think of it as: Dark and Light.

In the beginning is the darkness. I am high up on Dad's shoulders. My tiny legs wrap around his face, and I feel the stubble on his cheeks. We move from the lighted kitchen through the middle room toward the darkness of the parlor. No lamp is lit. The light bulbs on their paper candlesticks are extinguished beneath the cream-and-maroon silken shade. We walk a slow circle dance softened by invisible wool carpet roses far below.

"Dark," he says.

He moves back to the middle room, our living room, a halfway room toward the kitchen. His hands steady me and we move toward the light, a circle of brightness in the middle of the ceiling. It casts an odd gray-blue light on blue walls above white wainscoting and white enamel cupboards. We are so tall we are above the cupboards, almost as high as the chimney hole cover, a plate with its mandala painting of green and gold, of a shepherd, of trees and fields rimmed in fluted copper.

"Light," says.

Way, way down below, the turquoise linoleum swirls deep. We turn. Dad rides the waves as we rush out of the room and back to the dark parlor.

"Dark," he says again, reaching the parlor, completing a lemniscate path through the house. Roses.

"Light," Dad says to me, when we reach the kitchen once more. Shepherd on chimney.

We swing back along the whirling path. His pace quickens. We fly away from the light.

"Dark!" he says. "*Dark!*" I say, yelping as we run. He swirls, swings, and trotting to the kitchen, bounces me into gasped giggles.

"Light!" he says.

"*Light!*" I echo, and the excitement builds as he turns again.

"Medium," he announces to the middle room and pauses.

"*Medium!*" I sing out joyfully in my baby voice.

Mama and Dad laugh and clap. I see it—*medium*—the dark on one side, the light on the other, and I am happy and successful in between, with Mama and Dad lifting me up.

Tree Streets

"Okay. Start at the cemetery," Dad says. He guides the car toward the bridge.

I take a deep breath and begin, "Cherry, Locust…"

"Pear." He shakes his balding head. His hands grip the wheel tighter as he glides the heavy old Plymouth over the beautiful arched bridge. "Pear, Cherry, Locust," he reminds me. Mama sitting alongside him, smiles. Nods. Sometimes she encourages. Sometimes she corrects me.

The layout of my landscape begins here, at the Harrison Avenue Bridge, reciting tree streets as we cross the Roaring Brook Gorge. My world is contained in an area little more than a mile in any direction, circumscribing the distance that Mama and I can walk…except for Sundays, the one day we travel by car, and I have my lessons in the lay of our city.

Mama, Dad, and I are on our way *up the line*, as we always say, *going visiting*. We are on our way to see Mama's family, Auntie and Little Grandma in Dunmore, the small town bordering our city of Scranton—the one Mama grew up in. I am just tall enough to stand behind the driver's seat holding on to the chrome rail. I can barely see above the seat. Dad makes me recite, in order, the names of the east-west streets we cross going from our neighborhood all the way to Mama's hometown. In our world of streets and alleyways there is exquisite order. Tree streets run east-west, and avenues, named for presidents, run north-south. Reciting patterns of streets as we walk, ride buses, or ride in the car on Sunday is as much a part of life as counting the cars of each coal train we see.

"Pear," I begin again. "Cherry, Locust, Elm..."—that's where Uncle Bill lives—"Maple, Beech..."—where Grandma, Dad's mom, lives—"Birch, Willow, Alder..."— that's where we live—"Hickory" (the hospital), "River, Orchard, Hemlock, and then Moosic" (which is not a tree).

"Okay, so now we cross the bridge..." comes the prompt. "And what are the streets?"

Between the bridge's balusters I see the treetops as we finish the crossing. "Linden," I say. I have to think carefully, for here we cross into another neighborhood. The stoplight beyond the bridge at Linden Street turns red. I pause, take a breath, and continue the recitation, "Linden...Mulberry...Pine, Olive, Vine."

"Vine, Olive, *Pine*." The voices of Mama and Dad chorus from the front seat.

I grip the chrome rail tighter. I'm almost through all the names. "Vine, Olive, Pine. Myrtle, Poplar, Ash!"

That's as far as the recitation goes because we've reached the place where we follow the road to the right, out of this neighborhood, leaving the tree streets behind.

—

The streets tell one story of who we are, the story of an asphalt grid superimposed on the slopes of this mountain valley. The trains and waters tell another story. Trains pass over our streets on black iron trestles, they pass under our streets through tunnels, they are bridged over gorges and ravines and shuttled along the waters. Trains curve through the hollows, and where the trains are hindered by mountains or waters, more tunnels and bridges open the way for them to leave us and our neighborhood behind.

Our neighborhood is like an island between two bridges at the base of East Mountain. It is a woodland ravine sheltering houses from the Lackawanna Valley. Our hollow is a cleft that waters run through, and it is circumscribed by waters and rails. We are defined by the laundry we hang on clotheslines in our yards, by the people we pass on porches, or by the dead who sleep in the cemetery; by the trains that rumble through the hollow night and day, departing and coming home to this, the largest coal mining valley in the world.

We measure our neighborhood in walking distances. But if you were to ride an interstate highway through it, you would see how small it truly is. It would pass by in the blink of an eye, lost in a smoky haze. You'd never know about Mama and laundry, rags and old photos, fruit trees along fences and canning jars in cupboards. You wouldn't see furnace beasts in our basements or slate sidewalks in front of our houses, or minefires beneath it all, sending up smoke. You wouldn't know about any of it because you'd never have walked in our shoes.

And if I could lay out this world, sculpt hills and hollows as if it were some model railroad platform beneath a holiday tree, you could, like some fantastic giant, look at my neighborhood and see all of it at once: the mountain ridge and creek at the beginning of our hollow all the way to the brook, the tracks, and the cemetery at the hollow's end.

Look! I'd point. The creek begins up there at a slag pond on the mountain. The creek slips down into the woods, through a schoolyard, and drops between houses on a wooded slope. The water tumbles beneath rails and ties to create the very beginning of our hollow. Oily orange waters pool at the bottom of the slope, through the dumped tailings from the long-ago iron mills, but the creek cuts right through them, shining in sunlight, bumping over roots in the shade of a big willow tree. The creek crosses backyards of tall clapboard houses, where it slows for us children to race grass boats.

We children run with the creek as far as the culvert where the creek steals our shouts, carrying them along as it continues on in open air once again. Look how it passes the garment factory, how it tumbles past a small, tar-papered store whose Italian owner, Cungie, wears braids in a hairnet, and she smiles in a different language. The creek plunges under yards and disappears for a block or so. Look how the creek reappears one last time, tumbling into a bigger hollow. It pours down into the Stafford Brook, shushing of rain and rocks. Now you can see the train tracks above the brook, and how they curve up and away into this other hollow, disappearing around the bend toward the brook's source.

This confluence of waters and rails is the meeting

place of living and dead, the place where you can find our beginnings and endings. On this hill facing the brook, in a break in the scraggly beech wood, a grassy hill is hemmed in by a high iron fence. And inside, granite stones stand polished, rectangular, and regularly placed, naming our relations—those who held us and those we've only held in story. Spread across the hill in small clusters, the gravestones mark households, naming those who lived together and leave spaces for those who will join them. Here we trace our names incised in gray granite. Our names: first and last, passed on to us. These are our uncles, aunties, and cousins in this fenced-in yard. They laid rails, blasted coal, opened doors to the mines. They hauled and shoveled coal, and drank hard to blur hard living. Their hands pounded bread dough, watched it rise to pound it again. They held their children in the night, feverish from influenza, dying from diphtheria. And now they all lie, side-by-side, tiny headstones clustered behind large ones.

On this hillside the dead sleep. I imagine that their dreams drift down with the waters, float beneath the plank bridge, and past the tunnel. The quiet dances with the breeze that stirs and shakes the ribbons hung at each gravesite; the brook rolls over stones endlessly shushing, shushing.

But a train comes, breaking the stillness and the voice of the brook. A rattling rises like an angry wind. A squeal of wheel on rail, a wheel screaming, holding back. The dead might turn aside from their dreaming and observe the train emerging from the tunnel, grinding upgrade and around the bend. They would blink. What was that in life? They would try to remember this part of the story. Something about trains and coal. The train rumbles, its small chain of cars rattling, passing like a thunderstorm. It rounds the bend and fades away. Shushing waters take over and the dead go back to dreaming.

But the waters and rails move on, leading away from here. The two wind around each other, going downslope, sometimes as partners, sometimes swinging away and back, all the while descending into the great valley. The Stafford-Meadow Brook joins the Lackawanna River. The tracks join other tracks. Here water and steel must part. The river goes down between the mountains to an even grander river valley; the rails shuttle the filled coal cars up and out—black coal in black cars on silvery steel. This is where the known world ends.

Above the river, the pale blue curves of the West Mountains rise halfway to the horizon, making an edge that is as flat as paper. Those mountains bind us here. What's beyond them? Trees? More mountains? Towns?

The bear went over the mountain,

The bear went over the mountain…

we sing in Miss Shire's kindergarten class, circling round, holding hands, swinging arms.

To see what he could see,

To see what he could see…

Shout-singing, we pause in our circling. We lift our hands to shade our eyes and peer around.

To see what he could see!

"And *what* did he see?" asks the gray-haired teacher. She begins it for us in joyous shout-song:

He saw another mountain, he saw another mountain…

And that's how it is for us. Mountains are all around us. Mountains beneath our feet, beneath our streets, beneath our school. Mountains lined with veins of black coal, frozen into stone for all eternity until the industrious miners pick away, blast away, bring it all up to the surface. Break it, sort it, send it, then it's gone. Gone. Beneath our feet, empty veins drained of black coal, some filled with fire. Beside our homes, along our waters, rusty-pink rounded mountains of coal waste, the culm dumps, burn and smoke. A haze wraps the passive blue mountains that are as distant from our reality in the valley as the owners of mines and rails. The smoking culm mountains are the only true mountains—familiar, round, and real, they hulk beside our houses, line rivers and rails. They stand beside the breakers as conical black silhouettes, at night covered in blue flames.

Living along the sloping walls of the valley, we learn how easily things slip away from us. We have no control over the pull of slope. Our cars careen down our hills, braking, breaking, for they are old cars and might not stop. Once parked, our cars sometimes head downhill without us. We walk down into the valley to town, we walk to church sliding in our dress-up shoes, our toes squeezed and pinched. Our clapboard houses try to stand straight and tall, but they tilt. Waters trickle beneath them, basement walls sprout leaks and crumble, and the waters pull our houses downhill. Those of us living in the valley— the people—just stay, rooted like the trees in the shallow soil of the mountainside, wrapping ourselves around rocks and struggling to straighten up to the sun, trying to keep our balance.

But it is not always the waters racing downhill that make our houses lean. Mines also give incline to our houses. Beneath it all, beneath houses and streets, wooden pillars in mines rot, letting the surface sag. The mines cause us to stagger to our doorways, and struggle to open the doors. Mines make the gravy on the Sunday dinner plate slide to one side and stay huddled there. And sometimes our yards give way, leaving holes that go straight down to the mines.

The trains are not troubled by this. Beneath their rails there are no mines. The rails ride strong iron trestles or rim the valleys on firm beds. They tilt upward and out, heavy with coal. They strain the long grade up and out and disappear around the bend. Later they slip back down into the valley. The trains return home, rattling happily, coal cars empty, whistling a tune as if they've had a date with an unknown sweetheart. Where have they been? we wonder. We can't see beyond the mountain edge to where trains go—to docks, ferries, factories—to the streets of some other city. Streets named, perhaps like ours, for trees.

DREAM BRIDGE

I carry another view from those years—a darker view of the Sunday bridge crossing, from a vivid recurring dream that infused my childhood.

We are crossing the Harrison Avenue Bridge, over the deep gorge in a wide heavy car chromed in front and back. Dad is at the wheel; Mama is the front-seat passenger. I stand behind Dad's seat holding onto the chrome rail. All at once, the door on the driver's side swings open and falls off. My dad, mute with terror, is swept out of the car, out and tilting, falling downward over the bridge. Mama looks to the wheel in horror. I want her to take hold, but before she can, her door swings open and falls off and she, too, is swept out of the car and over into the gorge. The roof and sides of the car are next to go—swept away as if by hurricane winds. The car continues crossing the bridge on its own power. Small and alone in back, I still hold onto the chrome rail until it, too, is swept from my hands along with the backseat. The car finishes crossing the bridge and comes to the Linden Street stoplight. The light turns red, and I must take the wheel and get the car to stop before it reaches the intersection. I grab the wheel hoping I'll know what to do…

And there the dream ends.

Laundry

Each week I watch Mama in the dance of laundry. One time my view is from the basement, on the dark, damp cement floor. Mama is at the wringer washer and I am playing with small baking toys against the furnace chimney. Other times I am on the porch, or on the steps watching Mama haul laundry outdoors and upward to the clotheslines strung out across the yard. Sometimes I am in the backyard beneath the laundry lines, looking up at the sky. I am beside Mama as she sorts, as she irons. I am everywhere she runs with the laundry, from closets upstairs in the house down to the cellar, out to the grassy yard, and I have seen the laundry from every angle and slant of daylight. Mama paints my sense of the seasons of the year in damp or drying clothes, in the call of the washing machine, in the creak of pulleys and the slap of cotton in the wind. I can paint her portrait from every vantage point.

Of all Mama's work, laundry is the most silent. While she is wrapped up in it I cannot ask questions. She works steadily until late. She begins this way:

Mama comes downstairs to the dark, dank basement, holding her breath each time she steps from the top of the long, steep stairs. She balances the old, clothes-filled willow basket in front of her and begins the descent. Quickly, deftly, she avoids worn places on the stair step which would send her tottering. She makes the bottom landing with a bump and begins a new breathing rhythm: one without hesitation, one with purpose. Her worn leather-soled shoes slap across the tilted cement floor in a quick staccato, like drum and cymbal beat. Its rhythm offsets the wringer washer's song as it churns, slapping heavy muslin sheets: *Chum-chum, chum-chum.*

Mama crosses to the soapstone wash tubs, a permanent fixture of the old house. Once green and marbley-smooth perhaps, in the days half a century ago when the gas lights were lit, the wash tubs are now dull, slimy, but for the golden brass drain rings. She sets the willow basket atop the wringer washer and reaches for the washboard. Like the tubs, its wood is coated with slimy soap. She empties soiled clothes into the left tub, its strangely angled sides guiding the water downward, downward in sheets. She wets the clothes carefully, cold water only. Hot water is a luxury for shallow baths, greasy pots, and the white sheets now slapping syncopation to the washer song.

Behind her, the coal stoker furnace rumbles both summer and winter, heating the water in a small reservoir. And coal dust fills every surface of the basement, all the way to the coal bin at the far end. Coal ash is everywhere, too, and it rises upward through the cellar ceiling and through the cracks between the floorboards above.

Mama leans her body in its faded cotton dress against the tubs and reaches into the achingly cold water for my small clothing, dragging each piece upward to the ridges of the washboard. She scrubs hard—to force out all the dirt, the coal dust, the burden of parenting, the aloneness, the hard work. Why so many changes of clothes? She sighs in exasperation, though the small, dark bedroom closet and the small wooden wardrobe tell a different story. So few clothes. Few enough for the whole year to fit in these small spaces. While the washer chums, while she scrubs, while the furnace continues to crackle as it burns coal, she forgets today to look out the basement window, that one window beside the tubs.

She rinses once, swirling the clothes in gray reused water. "No sense wasting water," she says out loud. "That water bill has to be kept low." She unlocks the wringer and carefully swings it over the right tub. She lifts the clothes to the wringer, through its rollers and down. The wet, crushed fabric is guided by her hands away from the tub to the basket waiting on the floor. She is deft at feeding the wringer and guiding the flattened laundry to its basket. She must concentrate over the washer-song. Watch your fingers! she says to herself, watch your fingers! All the while the washer chums. *Chum-chum, chum-chum.*

Done and ready to head outdoors, Mama reaches for the basket and swings it onto her left hip. She takes four long strides to the basement door. Grunting, she pulls the heavy wooden door inward and pushes the screen door open with the basket. Sitting on the porch steps, I hear Mama coming, the willow basket creaking in rhythm on her hips as she sways, lifting the basket up each step. She sets out under the porch to begin the climb upward in an almost clockwise spiral: right around the metal pole, up the sidewalk, climb three tall cement steps, another right turn onto the cement landing and one more right turn to climb three wooden steps onto the porch floor, completing the circuit.

Mama passes me, the tattered edge of her worn full-skirted dress swings with her swiftness. She never grunts while carrying a load up the steps. She pants but does not grunt until she finally sets the wet load on the porch's gray, painted boards.

Mama looks at the porch and sighs. The porch floor, battleship gray, needs painting again. The railing, dark green, also needs paint. Although the railing is showing cracks, the porch floor is more important to do first: the gray paint is cheaper, and it will be easier to get a man to do a large, straightforward job.

Grayed birch clothespins rest in the cloth sack made from my old dress. While Mama plucks heavy wet clothes from willow baskets I walk little wooden clothespin people on the steps. "Pear, Cherry, Fig…" I name the tree streets as I walk my sturdy little people through the neighborhood.

Mama is at her finest out at the pulleys. The porch is her tower, from which she commands the long narrow yard below. She is outside, and she can breathe in the green from all down the yard, the adjacent yards, the woods, and the whole wooded hollow. The sky this day, though cloudy and swiftly changing, is her ally. She swings wet clothes up, clips, bends. Swings, clips, and looks up. Over and over Mama repeats this motif and smiles. When the load is hung, it's time for Mama to hurry back down to the basement to wring the next load through the rubber rollers while the round-bellied Maytag washer rocks and chums.

—

From the grass below, a sheet is a sail. I can look up past the cotton sheet to the blue, blue sky. The breeze leans back against the sailing sheet which fills—and snaps. Strong woven cotton threads laugh. Firm now—and Snap! The sheet commands the breeze beneath the clothesline, beneath the creaking iron pulley wheels at either end.

Green grass softly tickles my legs and face. Ants crawl to explore my hair and skin. I drift among the golden dandelion flowers and feel myself floating away into the blue sky on the cotton sail…

A *screeeech*. Mama reaches for the clothesline, hauls it in toward her, feeling the rope's woven V's scrape against her hand. The pulleys always rebel and screech and Mama is working quickly now to get the clothes in from the wind. All it takes is a strong wind and—disaster. A twisted line that she can't fix, that she can't rescue laundry from in changing weather. It requires a man with a ladder to climb up to the very top of the silver-painted pole, reach, unhook one pulley, untwist the parallel ropes, and gingerly hook the pulley back onto the pole without kicking out the ladder. Stranded clothes. Rain coming, wet sheets, only one set for each bed at daylight's ending.

♦ ♦ ♦

"Thunder and fine, straight rain." Mama lets go the curtain and shrugs her shoulders. "What a shame I can't get more laundry done." She sighs. "It'll be an ironing day."

Mama takes the wash baskets topped with clean sheets and shirts and sets up the ironing board next to the kitchen table. She lifts its silver-coated cloth cover to adjust the padding beneath made from folded old blankets. She fills the green glass spritz bottle with water from the faucet and sets the cork back in the bottle's mouth. She plugs the black cloth-covered cord into the wall socket above the kitchen table. Taking sheet after sheet onto the oilcloth table cover, she sprinkles droplets from the bottle, shaking it lightly over the cloth, as if seasoning it. The sweetly moldy water tempers the clean, warm laundry's fragrance with decay and resignation. The crisp dryness of the sheets melts. They become pliable and damp. All the sheets lie in a moist heap. She turns the iron's setting to "linen." The old iron clicks and groans as she spreads each sheet in turn before it, pounding the iron into the cloth, pounding wedges of smoothness into it until the cloth is hot and free of wrinkles.

She folds the sheets lovingly and lays them in the basket. I breathe the scent of warm cloth, dry—wet—dry again. A contenting scent. Mama, though impatient and fierce throughout a day's work, is quieter at this time, quieter at this task, her eyes cast downward to the iron, flashing as the iron's chrome catches and reflects the ceiling lamp's light.

◆ ◆ ◆

In late spring, with the windows open, yellowed window shades rise up on a breeze and drop! against the glass with a slap. Reaching...and...slap! The shade tries to push the lace curtains, but they hang limp and heavy, keeping the shade from rising. Mama sees it's time to clean curtains. Like the wallpaper, and the paperback books in the attic, and all the cottons in the house, they have yellowed, as everything does in coal-saturated air.

Only one day in the year, one late spring day full of clear sky and warm sunshine, Mama reaches behind the trunks and old *Life* magazines in the attic to pull out the curtain stretchers. She slides out the narrow lengths of wood, each as long as one of our rooms. She does so carefully, for wicked-looking nails stick out between black lines and numbers that mark the wood. Mama carries the curtain stretchers down two flights of stairs, and out and down another level into the yard. She assembles the frames, setting the wingnuts in place at the proper length, and leans the high rectangular frames against the edge of the porch floor above her. Mama climbs back indoors, two stories upstairs where, pair by pair, she takes down the lace curtains from each bedroom window. For her it is a dance as she sweeps into each of the rooms. Mama carries the yellowed lace back down to the basement. She washes the heavy curtains by hand, one at a time in the greasy basement tubs, squeezing, swishing, changing water. She lifts the heavy wet cotton gently so as not to tear the lace and slips each of the heavy lengths into the oval enamel pan, carrying it outside. Mama gently hangs each loophole of the picot edges over alternate nails.

I walk along the sidewalk. Red hollyhocks' prickly stems catch my curious fingers. Bumblebees drone around inside the hollyhocks' silky petals. I see the nails on the curtain frames jutting out so slender and sharp, and I run my fingers along their cool edges. Mama is smiling as she hangs the lace. I catch her joy and hang onto the full skirt of her flowered dress this clear day.

"Mama, why don't you hang the curtains on the lines?"

"That wouldn't work. Feel how heavy this is. They could tear." Mama hands me the edge of the curtain she's hanging. It flops over my hand, cold and wet. It looks like crocheted flowers spun onto a web of thick spidery threads. "And if I don't stretch these curtains they'll get all lopsided, and I couldn't hang them back on the windows."

"Did you make the lace curtains?"

"Me? No. They came from the lace factory downtown. Your godmother used to work there. A really big factory, with lots of women working."

"Making lace?"

"Yes. On machines in a big factory. This lace is famous…or was."

"Fancy?"

"No, famous. People all over knew about lace from Scranton."

"Why?"

"I guess it was fancy." Mama smiles and gives me a hug.

A Cup of Tea

A switching engine with a string of coal cars rims the mountain above me as I make my way down through the cindered lower alleyway past the houses in our hollow. The train rattles and rattles and screeches above me. White letters on black cars pass: Erie, Erie, Lackawanna…The coal cars take the coal away and come back for more. The horn blasts, echoes through the hollow, and dies away.

I pass through a blackberry patch, walk along the creek and willows, and shuffle through the grasses to an empty lot. There I climb the field of rocks that jut out from the grasses like steps and pass the blooming wild apple trees to the last alley behind Grandma's garage.

Nearly every day I walk to Grandma's house with Mama, or by myself. Along with my family's house, Grandma's house is the center of the world: part of me. Her house, like our house, is in our neighborhood at the edge of our city—a hollow between a steep hillside and a mountain.

I push the unpainted gate open and step down into her yard. The arbor frame, which held the grapevine, is falling down, and the coop and the dovecote are simply piles of wood. Old wooden barrels rot in the yard among the wild and untrimmed bushes and fruit trees. Over and over Dad has told me about how it used to be.

"During the Great Depression we had grapes and apples, a garden, and chickens—and even pigeons."

"Pigeons!"

"*Budacoo, budacoo,*" Dad coos deep in his throat, guttural. "That's the female call. *Budacoo, budacoo-wonk-wonk.* That's the male. You try it."

Grandma tells me, "He felt so bad about killing those birds. He always had a soft heart."

Grandma's yard is a terrible mess and so sad-looking, but today, in spring, the yard has flowers everywhere: mock orange, lilac, apple, and the bright red of quince along the fence. The gray, worn wood of the garage is hidden. Now everything seems happy.

Grandma's house, like nearly everyone's, needs paint. Her back porch scares me. It stands much higher than I do, and it has nothing but skeleton railings on it—nothing to keep us from slipping off. It stands above ground because our rocky hillside does not let us sink our basements in—although sometimes the coal mines underneath collapse and do that for us. At least in our hollow there are no mine fires below us as like there are in Minooka, but we breathe the smoke from their neighborhood anyway. At the back door, I freeze. I don't want to turn around in case I might be sucked backward off the edge.

Through the black mesh of the screen door I can see the big electric stove. It's late morning and Grandma hasn't had breakfast yet.

"Grandma!" I shout as I bang on the rough wooden frame of the door. I go into the kitchen and sit down at the table.

Grandma's kitchen smells like old meals: cabbage, tomato, and vinegar, sharp with sulfur and dusted with coal. Underneath all that, cloves and lilac perfume the house.

Behind me the refrigerator hums a cheerful, perfect fifth. I know if I open the refrigerator door, I'll find only a very few things inside: a bottle of milk, a pound of lard, a carton of eggs. Sometimes there are a few strips of bacon on a silver tray beneath the freezer compartment. Early in the month, there may be a few pork chops in the freezer. Grandma cooks more at the beginning of the month.

On the other side of the kitchen, in the corner, are two small cupboards. There is not much in them: a box of tea bags, a box of saleratus, a jar of honey. Sometimes it seems that Grandma is like Old Mother Hubbard. Poor Grandma. That's what we say. Grandma can't walk to get groceries. We aren't much better off, but at least Mama can still cook and dust our house and walk for groceries, and she does it for Grandma, too. The men we still have take turns shoveling coal into her furnace to keep her warm.

I lay my cheek down on the cool enamel surface of the table and peer into the length of Grandma's small house. It's so different from my other grandma's house—the house of my mama's mama, who is my Little Grandma because she is so small. In her house, the wainscoting is kept varnished and the walls painted. The doors all have pretty glass handles. Each dresser has a fresh, clean doily. Both the upstairs and downstairs in Little Grandma's duplex are taken care of. The lawn and gardens make her house seem like a mansion.

Here at Grandma's house in my own neighborhood, the yard is filled with rusting things from the past forty years. All the wallpaper is peeling and stained with coal. There aren't any glass door handles because there aren't any doors—just curtains hanging in the arched doorways between rooms.

I watch Grandma make her way to the kitchen, leaning on furniture as she comes. She wears her flowered housecoat with big buttons down the front, safety pins dangling from the placket edge so she won't lose them. Her stockings are turned down below her swollen ankles. She smiles to find me resting my head on the table. Grandma leans over, and putting her arms around me, squeezes me in her hug with a sweet grunt.

"Would you like some tea, honey?"

I nod.

"How is your mama today?"

"Okay, I guess. She told me to tell you that she'll come over later."

Grandma depends on my mama, her daughter-in-law, to help her clean her raggedy house, and she counts on me to walk to the corner store to get the supplies she needs. Like tea bags.

Grandma sets her cup and saucer down on the table end nearest the stove and places my favorite cup beside hers. It's a thick porcelain cup like the ones at the Woolworth's lunch counter—a perfect white bowl of a cup with a perfectly round porcelain finger ring. Mama says it's like railroad ware. "Heavy, like the kind used on trains. They don't tip over so easy." Mama got to ride trains when she was a girl. The railroad that Grandpa worked for in the shops fixing locomotives gave Grandpa's family free rides.

The cup is edged in rose red. The heavy saucer beneath it is edged in green. None of Grandma's cups or plates match. None of the furniture in her house matches, either. Most of it has arrived on the Goodwill truck. The only things that match are her knick-knacks on a wooden shelf: pairs of saltshakers shaped like pineapples, penguins, a Dutch boy and girl.

Sometimes I wish Grandma were part of a pair—that I had a Grandpa, too. When I asked Dad, he told me his dad died in the 1940s. Dad was sad about it, because he came back from war to say goodbye, but didn't make it in time. I knew my other grandpa—who had no legs because he got poisoned working on locomotives—but he died. Mama says we're just a valley of widows, but I tell her we still have kids, too.

A few things in Grandma's house are her very own—pretty things—a few pieces of silverware, some really nice dessert dishes, and an oval frame holding an old photograph of her parents dressed in beautiful, old-fashioned clothing. Her mama wears the kind of dress women wore in the 1800s. The faces from that photograph are in each piece of jewelry Grandma's family gave to her: her locket, a choker, and a few hat pins. The people in the photo seem so fancy and look at us in a happy way. Neither Grandma, my parents, nor I have ever had such a fancy photo taken of us. Sometimes I stare at the photo, wishing I could see those people in color, for real.

I used to like sitting in the rocker by the radiator at Grandma's house as I listened to Dad or my uncles talk. With just Grandma and me, I like sitting here at the kitchen table, facing the stove, watching Grandma's broad back as she cooks, as she moves, so slowly.

Grandma sets aside the hard-boiled egg pan from the burner and puts on another small one to heat water. The smells of old meals rise strongly whenever an electric coil is heated, followed by a strange, sweetish smell of lye.

"You know, I'll give you some cameo tea," Grandma tells me.

"Cameo tea?"

"Girls like you can't drink regular tea. It's too strong. This'll be mostly milk with a little flavoring of tea."

Grandma brings the small water pan to the table, filling her cup. She reaches across the table and fills my cup only halfway.

"Watch out," she says gently, "this is very hot."

From a jar high on the corner cupboard, she takes a tea bag with a rose on the paper label. After dipping the bag in her cup, she dips it in mine. She pours milk into my cup to fill it and stirs in some sugar.

One time, when Grandma used the cup to serve my mama tea, the teabag broke in Mama's cup, and Grandma said, "We can read our fortunes!" Grandma had a crumbling booklet from the 1920s that told what kind of fortune you would have by the shape the tea made in the bottom of the cup. The booklet also told what dreams meant. Grandma sent me to get it from her bedroom. Mama sat quietly at the table and smiled to herself. She didn't believe in any of that stuff.

After swirling the leaves in the thick porcelain cup, Grandma waited for them to settle, and we peered inside. "It's a bird," she called out. "Nooo, it's a teapot. Maybe we're supposed to have more tea."

When we looked up bird, it said something about travel. Teapot said something about having guests.

Mama looked up like she was trying to decide about it. "I like the bird one," she said. It made her smile, and then she drank her tea.

For each of us, Grandma prepares a small plate with a hard-boiled egg. Knowing that I don't like the rough sandpapery feel of eggshells, she peels mine, too. The egg looks small in her big hands, and her fingers move stiffly. It's hard for her to do this, but she does it for me anyway.

Grandma lifts her cup. "Now you can sip your tea like this…hold your pinky up," she demonstrates. "Just like the blue bloods." She smiles and sips. I do the same. It's so grown up.

"Grandma, what are 'blue bloods'?"

Grandma gets a wistful look on her face. She smiles. "They're the rich people, honey." She pauses. "Not like us. But we can pretend, anyway." She sips her tea and holds out her little finger. I look her in the eyes and do the same. Her blue eyes are lighter than my dad's.

"Grandma, were your dad's eyes blue?"

She nods and looks down, thinking.

"Tell me, again, Grandma, about your dad's mom in Germany, the one who died..."

"But for the blink of an eyelid, you wouldn't be here. Or me."

I hold my breath. Now she'll say it...

Grandma sips her milky tea. "My grandma in Germany died. My father's mother was being laid in the grave. My grandfather and the children were there. He was taking it hard because he really loved her. But before they closed the coffin, her husband wanted one last look at her. He leaned over to kiss her...and he saw her eyelids move."

"He saw her eyelids move?"

"He saw her eyelids move. They fluttered, like this," Grandma closes her eyes and blinks them. "She wasn't dead. The doctor couldn't find a heartbeat or breath. There they were, at the funeral and grave and all..."

"And she wasn't really dead!" I finish for Grandma.

"No, she wasn't. She was almost buried alive. And..." Grandma pauses for both of us to consider, "...my father was born after that."

Grandma sips her tea. She lifts her face but does not see me. Her pale blue eyes look beyond the chrome-edged table, beyond the thin and skewed walls of the house, into some other field of time.

Old Photos

"Remember," I hear Auntie say, a firm, but gentle command. "You're old enough now to remember your life. You're young, but you're growing. These are your people. You have to remember."

I am sitting on the maroon couch in my Italian-American grandparents' parlor, sandwiched between Mama and Auntie. On their laps are photo albums of crumbling black paper, filled and bulging with sepia scenes of people facing us. Always photos of people, never of places and things. Some crossed oceans. Most of the people in the photos except for Mama and Auntie and their mama are gone.

We look at a postcard photograph of a little girl and a baby sitting on a pony. Mama is the older one sitting solemnly in a white dress, white stockings, and high-top shoes. She is five years old. Auntie is the little one dressed in white lace whom Mama holds in front of her. The baby's dark eyes are bright and curious. Mama taps her finger next to the postcard. "Look at this one."

"Why were you on a pony, Mama?"

"Oh, a man came up to our house, right out here, and

offered to take our picture for five cents. So Ma and Tha let us! See, we put on white dresses! And the man put the pony right on our sidewalk."

"A horse on the sidewalk? Why Mama?"

"Oh, there were horses and wagons on the street all the time—the milkman, the iceman, the ragman, the tinker… but this one came right on the sidewalk next to the house with the pony so we could sit on it. A pony ride on the sidewalk!"

"Mama, what's a ragman?"

"He was a ragman. He would blow his horn and Ma would get out our rags. He'd pay her for them and…"

"Oh, I remember that horn," says Auntie shaking her head. "So loud—it didn't sound like *anything* else…"

Mama passes the photo album to me. I look at it again. "So you sat on a pony and…"

"Let me see that," Auntie studies the photo, then shouts, "That's no pony!"

She stares at it and makes a face. "It's a *mule*!"

A *mule*! We laugh.

Auntie pauses. "You know, this street out here has changed. No more street peddlers…no mansions."

"Mansions?"

"Yeah. Across the street."

I look out through the curtain sheers and all I see are car repair shops, and behind them, piles of culm.

Before I can begin a question, Mama nods. "The coal barons' houses."

"Why aren't they there now?"

Auntie looks at me. "They left."

"The houses left?"

"No, the mine owners. They got their money from the mines and they left and the houses got torn down."

We turn back to the photos. "Look, there's Cousin Jenny from Buffalo."

Mama points to a photo of a little girl with dark eyes and dark, glossy hair, looking out at us, a little sadly. A huge, white, bow halos her head. "Do you remember when we rode the train to Buffalo?" Mama asks Auntie.

"Oh, that was a long trip."

Mama nods in agreement. "That was a long time ago. And oh, I got *so* sick on that train. It went so fast."

I'm puzzled by this. "But Mama, you like trains."

"Yes, I do." Mama sighs. "I wish I could ride one again."

"Why don't you?"

"Oh! We could never afford to take a train trip. Not now. Even then. We all went because our Tha, your grandpa, worked for the Erie, rebuilding coal locomotives. He got free passes for all of us. But that was a long time ago. They don't do that now. There's hardly a train to take passengers to Buffalo now."

"Why?"

"The trains are mostly gone, honey," Auntie says gently. "Most people travel by car." She pauses. "You know, a lot of men used to ride the boxcars, too, looking for work. Tha always told us if any tramps came to the door for food to give them some. They even had their own marks they'd put out there on the corner, by the gate, to tell all the others that we were a good house to go to."

"When Tha got free tickets, we went all the way to Niagara Falls. Just think! It was so *big*. And we got so wet," says Mama.

Auntie laughs. "Not me. I stayed in the car."

"You stayed in the car?"

"Jenny's parents had a real automobile. I was so excited to be in an automobile, I wanted to stay in it all day. So they left me there. I didn't care about any falls."

Auntie looks at Mama and smiles. "Do you remember when Tha used to make us pick dandelions for wine? We had to pick so many, over in the fields by the railroad shops." Auntie turns to me. "Not a lot of juice comes out of the dandelion flower, you know."

Mama looks at Auntie but doesn't really see her. Her eyes look back a long way, and then she nods. "Oh, and *then* he'd make us push the press and squeeze out those flowers. Such a bitter smell—a sweet one, too."

"Mama, you had to make wine for Grandpa?"

"Oh yes. Tha would make us work. We'd push that press in the basement...it's something that horses used to do. And here we were, just kids, pushing this big wooden beam around and around..."

"And we never got paid. Can you imagine? We were *kids* and thought it was *fun*." Auntie laughs. "*Mules'* work, that's what it was."

"Look there," says Auntie. She points to a photo of a girl, perhaps eight years old, with black bobbed hair and a forehead hidden by bangs. The girl wears a white dress and stockings, but the stockings are crumpled at her ankles, leaving her knees and shins bare.

"Who is it?" I peer over at the dark-eyed girl.

"It's me, you silly. Uncle Charlie took the picture. *My* Uncle Charlie—not *your* Uncle Charlie. He took lots of them of me. I was his favorite. That was my first communion dress. I was supposed to be all dressed up. I wanted to be a *flapper*," Auntie laughs, "so I rolled my stockings down."

I look at Auntie. Beneath her graying curls her eyes shine. "So *my* Uncle Charlie…"

"Your Uncle Charlie is my brother. *My* Uncle Charlie is my dad's brother. That makes him your great uncle."

Here we go again. Every time we look at the photos we have to claim our uncles and aunts. First names are used over and over and it all gets so confusing.

"So…there are two Aunt Anges, right? Is one *mine*?"

"No…they're both *mine. Your* great-aunts. Aunt Ange On-the-Hill and Aunt Ange Down-the-Street."

"And Aunt Millie?"

"Well, there's Aunt Millie From-the-Hill and Aunt Millie from Rome, New York. But they're both *my* aunts."

"One name that's never worked is William. Bill. Even Willie." Auntie shakes her head.

Now Mama shakes her head sadly. She looks at me. "There were two babies—my brothers—we named Willie. Both were born after me. I held them. They died."

"Why, Mama?"

"Oh, I don't know. One was rickets."

"Rickets?"

"His bones didn't grow right…he couldn't stand. He was two when he died."

Mama looks at me searching for more of an answer. "It's a disease that little ones can get if they don't get the right food." Mama sighs. "I don't know. Maybe my ma didn't have enough milk to nurse him."

"And Grandpa's younger brother who came from the old country," Auntie shakes her head. "He was named William."

"What happened?"

"He went into the mines when he was fifteen and there was an accident. That's when they just came to America. We don't have a photo of him. And so, when Grandpa's family had another baby in America, they named him William." Auntie turns the page and pauses thoughtfully before a photo of a man in a pale uniform and cap. He wears a broad black belt and creases in his pants. He stands between Grandma and Grandpa but towers over them. The man's eyebrows are dark and strong like theirs, but his face is different: broad and open with happiness. In the photo, Grandma and Grandpa's faces looked troubled and they stand stiffly.

"Do you remember *my* Uncle Bill?" Auntie asks me. "He was my age." Auntie answers herself, "Oh no. You were born after the war."

◆ ◆ ◆

Years later a relative finds an article about a mine accident, but it has our grandfather's uncommon first name, and as far as we know, his leg was never broken in a mine accident, nor did he work in a mine.

Then I remembered William. Fifteen, underaged. To protect my immigrant great-grandfather who worked for the mining company, the accident would have been reported under the older brother's name.

Provisions

Blueberries

"She only came up to here on me."

Mama points to her collarbone to show me how small her grandma was. My Italian grandma, my mama's mama nods. They lean over the parlor couch, Mama pointing out the photo of herself, Dad, and Great-Grandma. Mama is a small woman. Her mama is smaller and her mama's mama is smaller still.

I look at the black and white photos of the white-haired woman at Mama's wedding—a stoop-shouldered, tiny old woman wearing a shiny black taffeta dress that falls to her ankles. She is dressed in black because her husband died and she'll never wear colors again. Her hair, like my grandma's, is thin and bound back on her head in a bun. The photo in black and white is of a woman in black and white, but with words, mama fills the photo with colors of rosy dawn and golden tea in a white porcelain cup. She tells me, "Great-Grandma was sweet, always sweet. She rose before dawn and drank a cup of chamomile tea every day. That's why she was so pleasant," Mama reminds me. My grandma purses her lips and turns her head side to side in agreement. Her small chin and dark eyes look like Great-Grandma's face in the photo—like my mama's face. Mothers and daughters.

"She baked bread in an outdoor coal oven in her back-yard," says Mama. "People did that years ago." I imagine an outdoor oven of rusty brick, and when the black iron door is opened, golden brown loaves are slid out by the dozens.

"My grandma made those sheets you sleep on," Mama reminds me. "She even bleached the muslin white in her backyard." I've seen and felt the white sheets with hand-sewn hems of the tiniest, neatest stitches. Sheets so thick they have lasted half a century, white and cool on our beds, white and sailing on our clothesline.

"Grandma walked up the mountain every day in blue-berry season and picked blueberries. She carried thirty quarts of blueberries on her head and walked five miles down the valley to market to sell them at dawn."

"Thirty quarts?"

"Thirty canning jars' worth of blueberries."

"On her head?" So many berries. So much blue!

"On her head. In a pan. It was a way to make money here. Lots of people picked berries and sold them by the rail lines."

Blueberry season. The wild July sky is filled with white, rounded clouds. Summer turns and ripens. Mama, Dad, Grandma, and I must gather what we can before cicadas sing a song of saws. On a Sunday afternoon, we have come by car up the mountain and walked the trail along the dou-ble set of train tracks that skirt our hollow. The shiny silver rails creak in summer heat. Peering between them I can see thick iron spikes that hold the rails to the rough wooden ties, spikes with raised numbers on their heads, naming the year each was driven in by a gandydancer. I move in closer wanting to touch the raised numbers that call to my fingers, but Dad steers me away from the rails though no trains are coming.

We head away from the tracks, down a dry path between low, gray stones. Before us a field of blueberry bushes spreads low over the mountain's bones. Though berries are everywhere, they hide beneath long, pointy leaves. A brush of a hand reveals berries, hues of ripe blue and unripe rose on green. Blueberries are magic, free food.

"Are you sure you know which ones are blueberries?" Mama asks me. I nod and Mama sets to her picking. Mama picks berries quickly and with purpose, eating hardly any. With ease, she fills her tall juice can and empties it into the pail.

Mama doesn't like gardens, but she doesn't seem to mind picking berries for pie. She eats wild, picks dandelions for salad out of the yard for lunch every day.

I'd rather fill pans of blueberries and be a hero, walking like my great-grandma did, down the valley to a downtown market with horses and wagons in the streets, surrounded by trains to carry the fruit from our hands to someplace far away.

Tomatoes

On Sundays in fall, Mama, Auntie, and I walk beneath the horse chestnut and catalpa trees, beneath the Norway and silver maple trees that line the streets in Mama's hometown. Hidden among the green leaves are the semaphores of autumn's coming: spiny horse chestnut husks, cigar-shaped catalpa seed pods, and the wings of green maple seeds.

We have put away our summer garments with their pastel pinks, yellows, blues. The white shoes, purses, hats, and gloves are put away in dark corners of closets and mothballed trunks until they are revived at Easter next year. I don't like it. When I asked Mama why we have to wear dark clothes she just shook her head. "Not after Labor Day," is all she said. It has something to do with church and tradition, but no one's ever been able to explain it. The church calendar we hang in our kitchen is striped with pink fast days and white feast days, but nowhere on it is a marking for putting away bright clothing or taking it out again. And when we go to the garment mills for winter coat seconds, the only colors are dark.

Sundays are for visiting relatives. We have relatives on this hill, along each of the streets, and we have relatives of relatives to visit, too. They are double-decker families, stacked on top of one another in first and second-floor flats. The houses are nearly all stucco, tall, and crowded together so closely you can reach a mop out a window of one house and almost wash a neighbor's window.

All the old relatives are home, or are at least nearby. No one has a car. We can find our aunts, uncles, and cousins ready to receive us at their doors. They are quick with offerings of coffee and sweet breads. Or, if they're not at home, all we have to do is walk around the corner to some other family house and find them there. Visiting, too.

Today we go to the house of the old uncles, brothers from Italy, Zi' Ming and Zi' Pepp, and their wives, Zi'

Marigue and Aunt Millie. Unlike all the other members of my mother's large family, this branch has retained the Zi'—for a beloved old man or woman who could be a very distant relative. I am still trying to figure out the Zi'. If I ask, "Why is his name Zi' Ming?" Mama answers first.

"Because he's an uncle—Ming."

Auntie helps. "And his name is Dominick. Domingo."

"And Zi' Pepp…is Uncle Pepp?"

"Well, his name is Joseph. Yeah, well, actually, Giuseppe—Pepp," says Auntie.

"But you say, Zi' Marigue. She's not an uncle…"

"No—she's an aunt—a Zi'."

"A Zi'?"

Both Mama and Auntie hesitate, searching for an explanation for me.

Auntie tries first. "Zi' means uncle or aunt."

"So Aunt Millie is Zi' Millie," I offer.

"No!" Mama answers forcefully and laughs. I wonder if I've said something wrong.

Auntie explains, "Aunt Millie was born in America—she's not a Zi'."

What Mama and Auntie don't say is that with the old ones called Zi', a sense of deep connection to their homeland is there, and if they speak English at all, it's with a heavy accent.

When the steam locomotives used to haul the coal from the valley, the old uncles worked in the railroad shops. By day they walked downhill to work, building and rebuilding big, black locomotives, and after work they walked these flagstone sidewalks home, their work clothes coated in blackness, their bodies covered in fragments of their beloved engines.

At home, the old uncles shed their blackened coveralls for their hair-netted housewives to clean while they put on frayed work clothes and went straight to the tiny garden patches in their tiny yards, leaving the aunts to click their tongues.

The steam locomotives were all sold for scrap metal just before I was born, and the railroad replaced them with square-faced or cone-nosed diesels. The old uncles don't work anymore—except in their gardens. With shiny, clean-shaven faces, they dig in the yard. Their hands, their strong fingers, plunge into soil like thirsty plant rootlets seeking water. The old uncles seek soil in their hands. Their hands move tenderly. Their faces crease in smiles. They are at peace.

In the upstairs and downstairs kitchens of the stucco houses, old aunts preside over spicy sausages and tomatoes cooking down in deep pots, fat, slippery pastas. Wiping the oilcloth-covered tables, they complain that their husbands are out in their gardens again. Their husbands are grow-ing tomatoes, beans, peppers, basil—Aay! It's too much, the old aunts complain to the stoves and enamel counters. You'll grow too much, they say to their husbands, though actually speaking to cupboards. It's too much! It is the women, after all, who do the canning, and they hate the gardens.

I am outdoors in Zi' Ming's yard. His garden patch is so

tiny I can only walk around it, not through it, to admire how tall the tomatoes grow.

"Here!" Zi' Ming calls to me. "Here Bella! You like tomatoes?" He is on his knees before his tomato patch; his green work pants and shirt hang loosely on his lean frame. I move in close beside him and look at his patch.

His tomato plants are hung like criminals, bound with rags to tall wooden stakes, bound by pieces of Aunt's housecoats. Singly, each plant could be a crucifix, but there are so many so close together, the patch is really a forest of tomatoes ripening on their stems. Plum tomatoes droop like huge water droplets hiding behind leaves. They look like Zi' Ming: long-faced, long-nosed, quiet, in their frosty pink-red skins. They are bound up, dry tomatoes. You cook them less when you make a sauce, so you don't cook away the flavor. Zi' Ming thinks that's the way tomatoes should be.

Zi' Ming's tomatoes are not at all like my grandpa's tomatoes. His plants sprawl on ash-covered soil and yellowed newspapers. They command the ground like he does. They are round and fat. They are juicy and brilliant orange-red. You cook them down a long time to create a sauce, to create that flavor. My grandpa patrols the brick paths he has laid in his garden, his garden as large as two city lots! When Grandpa takes me into his garden I have to trot to keep up with him, and I have to stay on the brick paths until he invites me to leave them, and then step carefully around the sprawling tomato stems on the ground. Grandpa has broad shoulders and broad, strong hands that pinch my cheeks before he kisses them and makes me blush. My grandpa overshadows everyone, especially my Little Grandma.

"Here!" Zi' Ming calls to me gently. "You like basil? The basil, see?" Zi' Ming whispers, cradling the bright green leaves out to me. "She like to grow lika dis—wit' tomatoes, see?"

I nod. He crouches beside me and lets me touch the square-stemmed plants. The air fills with basil's fragrance—the sweet perfume of Little Grandma's ravioli— the sweet, nose-tingly smell in the Italian store that rises to the cheeses and salamis strung from the ceiling. I am so happy to be with Zi' Ming and his basil. I want to stay with him and be in the garden all afternoon, but Mama calls me indoors to Aunt Millie's downstairs kitchen.

In the dim room, Mama and my aunts sit around Aunt Millie's table, their coffee cups filled. The old aunt pulls a fruit-speckled curtain aside and peers out the window.

"Why does a man want to do this?" she asks with a scowl. "He plays wit' dirt!"

The other women smile and shake their heads, but I cannot laugh. I like Zi' Ming's and Grandpa's gardens. I like the tomatoes, the ashes, the soil, the basil. I like the blue canning jars in both my grandmas' houses filled with tomatoes. Can't they see how beautiful it all is—the plants, the shine on the tomatoes, green stems and starry caps, the red globes—can't they see it?

"You want soda?" the old aunt asks me. I nod. She pours the thick, dark cola into a small, slender glass for me.

"Canning. Phew! I'm done wit' canning," says the old aunt. She complains: "Always growing tomatoes. Tomatoes, tomatoes. Too many tomatoes!" She throws up her hands in supplication. "Why so many? We can buy tomatoes in cans at the stores."

"Oh, they taste better," someone dutifully replies.

The old aunt faces the guests. "Yah, they taste better. But too many! Look at me—I'm sixty-t'ree years old. I don't want to can no more. Phew! I'm done wit' canning!"

I look to my mama. She is nodding and smiling. Is this what she thinks, too? Is this why she won't let us have a garden?

When it's time to go home, Zi' Ming digs out basil plants for me so Mama can plant them in a pot. Aunt Millie rolls them in wax paper and hands them to me.

"Here," says the old uncle. He fills a brown paper bag with long, pointy hot peppers. Yellow, green-yellow, orange-red. He bends down to plant a kiss on my cheek. We smile at each other. Mama and I take the color treasure home.

◆ ◆ ◆

The women of my mama's family tire of canning, but Mama still does it with Grandma, my dad's mom.

"Grandma and I are finishing with the tomatoes for now, so you'll have to go outside when the jars are ready. You know you can't be here when we're canning." Mama sends her words towards me across the kitchen.

Steam rises from the white enamel kettle on the black

surface of the stove above me. On the back burners two large, speckled blue kettles rattle and hiss. I am in the perfect place to watch the beautiful blue flames of the burners.

"Them are good tomatoes from your father," Grandma says to Mama as she nods slowly. She cleans her big hands and wipes them dry on her apron.

"Yeah, Tha grows them good."

Grandma, Dad's mom, is so much taller than my mama and anyone in Mama's family. And unlike the dark hair and dark eyes in Mama's part of the family, Grandma's family is fair and blue-eyed. Her short, dark blonde hair is permed and tightly curled—something Mama would never do.

Though she was born here, in America, Grandma's family came from Germany just before she was born. Grandma is slow in her movements and speech, but she knows a lot. She even knows how to make sweet jelly from tomatoes.

Behind me, against the opposite wall, the cutting boards and oilcloth covering the wooden table are wet with thin, red juice and the remains of cut tomatoes. Mama and Grandma are moving swiftly, cleaning the work surface, and wiping it dry. They lay strips of old sheets on the table and turn to the crate of jars on the blue linoleum floor. They must now bring these jars to the sink and wash them. At the other end of the table, near the kitchen door, three wooden bushel baskets with tomatoes from Mama's dad rest on the floor, their wire hands raised upward in a gesture of praise.

One basket holds green tomatoes, each carefully wrapped in newspaper. Mama will let these rest and ripen over the next few weeks. This day's canning tomatoes have come from the other baskets—one nearly full and the other in which only a few remain. The tomatoes are the most beautiful orange-red. Their caps are deep green and crackle to the touch like crepe paper. I long to feel the tomatoes, cool and round in their smooth skins. I reach into the full basket and squeeze one. It splits as I lift it, spilling juice and seeds on my dark red dress, but not on the floor. I lick the opening in the fruit and suck some seeds from it. Mama doesn't see, so I place the tomato back into the basket tucked among the others.

The timer bell on the top shelf of the stove rings—the first batch of sterilized jars in the blue-speckled kettle has just finished boiling.

"It's time, Mom," Mama says to her mother-in-law, and she pushes the table away from the wall and brings it nearer to the stove.

To me she says, "Okay, outside."

From the outside, the back porch screen mesh darkens the scene. Canning comes mostly in sounds: steam hiss, gas hiss, metal kettles rattling. Thickening tomato splats. Glass jars rocking. The click of metal against the glass neck of a jar as Grandma clamps the jar lifter to its quarry and holds aloft each boiled jar above the kettle, draining the hot water out without splashing the gas flames or herself. She swings and brings the jar to the cloth-padded table, setting it upside-down with a dull thump. Grandma slowly swivels on her heel six more times and brings each jar gently to the sheeting.

Mama lifts the heavy, white enamel pan from the front

burner and sets it beside the hot jars. She reaches for the
white ladle and dips it into the speckled kettles boiling
water, a purification. We have Holy Water fonts in each
room of the house for dipping our fingers and blessing ourselves. "In the name of the Father, the Son, and the Holy
Ghost…" Does Mama have a prayer to say for ladles?

"Okay, Mom, ready," Mama says.

Clamping and lifting the first jar right side up, Grandma
sets the funnel in. Mama ladles the partially cooked tomato
into the jar and fills it just to the bottom edge of the funnel. Grandma lifts the funnel out and sets it into another
jar while Mama checks the rim of the filled jar to see that
no tomato has touched it. She has the bottom edge of her
apron ready to wipe any spills along the side of the jar,
and a cloth dipped in boiling water to clean the jar rim.
Mama fits on the rubber ring and screws on the zinc cap.
Grandma finishes the job of tightening the lids all the way
down. Grandma picks up the jar lifter and grips the first
filled jar. She lifts it into the air, swivels and slides it into
the big blue kettle. Each filled jar plunges into the boiling
water with a *ploosh* sound, and the water changes its tune
from a rolling boil to a vibrating hiss.

After the kettle is filled with sealed jars, Grandma turns
up the flame and gets the jars rocking. She sets the timer at
the top of the stove and turns back to the table to ready the
second batch and begin tomato jelly. Grandma slices lem-
ons into the thinnest slivers, turning them into pale shards
of stained glass. In times between filling jars Grandma
mixes sugar, ginger, clove, and lemon with tomato and sets
it to cook in a tall pot on the front of the stove.

Behind me, beyond the porch, late rains begin to fall.

The kitchen windows fog, and rich steam of tomatoes comes out the screen door to greet me. When the tomato jelly boils enough to stand a spoon Grandma fills jelly glasses, waiting for them to cool before preparing their paraffin seals. From a small pan, Grandma pours a film of clear liquid onto the jelly. The wax soon cools and turns milky white. Grandma then lifts and tilts each glass side to side to seal the jelly in its winter beds. Mama meanwhile reaches into the breadbox, pulls out the remains of a loaf of her bread, and slices a piece. With the slice, she wipes clean the jelly left in the pan and hands it to me.

I am richly satisfied. The bread—the red jam—the sealed jars cooling on the table. Our tomato is put up. Our sweet, thick jams are finished. We will have fruit this winter. When this long gray afternoon is over, clear and turquoise glass jars filled with orange-red tomatoes will rest on the top shelf of the basement cupboard next to the jars of canned peaches from my Italian grandpa's yard. And in a small glass-windowed cupboard built into the wall next to the coalben, low, wide jars of tomato jelly will line the shelves next to jars of grape jelly Mama and Grandma put up earlier this harvest season. In the dark of winter, when the furnace roars and hisses and demands more coal, I will look for leaks in wax lids—the purple or red dribbles of sweet jam juice so I can sneak a taste.

Groceries

Just about any Saturday of the year, mama will take me along to get groceries.

"Come on, we're going to the store," is what she says as she reaches into her closet for her big, black pocketbook.

"To Pete's?"

"No, to the *store*. To the A&P."

"Pete's is a store. And it's closer."

Mama steps out onto the porch before answering. "Yes, it's a store, and it has some food, but it's only a corner store. Pete does sell mostly cigarettes and candy. We've got to get groceries."

Pete's yard meets the alley farther up the hill and is filled with flowers. His little tar paper store sits on the corner, a cigar box building tacked onto his tar paper house. Pete sells mostly cigarettes and candy. Teenagers use the chance to "buy for their family" though actually trying a pack of cigarettes in the alley. Most of the day Pete stands at his tall, brass cash register sandwiched in a tiny space between the rows and rows of cigarette packs on the wall behind him and the candy-filled glass counter in front. Whenever he watches us kids in the store, he purses out a breathy whistle, and he never says a greeting to any of us—ever. The silver stubble on his broad face echoes the silver close-shaved crew cut on his head. If Frank Sinatra comes on the radio that perches near the ceiling of the store, Pete turns his back on the big picture window and aims his whistle down the length of the dark store, trilling like a lark, his cigar stub held with precision between thumb and forefinger. He never seems to trust us kids. While he trills his whistle, only his eyes move—following every move we make at the candy wall or the ice cream freezer farther back in the store. Beyond the freezer, in the very back of the store, beside the cheese and meat cooler and scale, is a mysterious door that leads to Pete's mother's kitchen. We never think of Pete as having a home. He seems to live in the store, or just disappear into the night like wisps of smoke from his cigar.

Every so often Mrs. Welch from next door sends me with a note and dollar bills up the hill to Pete's to get her groceries. Waiting for Pete to gather all the items on Mrs. Welch's list, I look at the penny candies inside the glass counter: candied bacon, striped brown, pink, and white like Neapolitan ice cream; candy dots on long strips of paper that looked like cash register paper; hard black pillows of myrrh-flavored sen-sens in wax paper bags; chalky candy cigarettes; green gummy spearmint leaves coated in sugar crystals; twisted licorice ropes. Above the door, up against the white tin ceiling, Pete has hung corn cob pipes, fishing line, hooks, and sewing needles. Pete has cat food, light bulbs, saltpetre for homemade volcanoes, punk sticks, squirt guns, yo-yos, and paddle balls. He even has chalky black tablets which, when set on fire, make a crude oil-smelling foam that snakes in ashy black.

Near the door, Pete has bottles of soda in wooden crates. When we buy our sodas, we can sit on the outside step and drink them dry. Then we put the bottles back into the crates inside the store and collect the return money. We can buy a fair amount of penny candy by scouring the hedges outside the store and around the street corner for castaway bottles. Pete then opens the cash register without a word and hands us our coins, which we gratefully spend right on the spot.

I cast a long backward glance at Pete's store as we enter the alleyway, still hoping Mama will change her mind, but she's got my hand now, and she's quickening her stride. "Pete's too expensive," Mama replies. "And I've got coupons for the A&P. Come on!" Mama walks faster still.

After the two-block walk through alleys, we cross the cindered field to the A&P. Its huge glass windows reflect popcorn clouds floating over flat patches of blue sky. Mama opens the first metal door for me. I scoot in, then turn to open the second metal door for her. We are greeted by roars and screeches, and coffee scents the air. Mama separates a grocery cart from the horizontal stack beside the windows and steps aside so I can be the driver this time. The netted chrome wires gleam, each one a tiny mirror reflecting the outside sky. The handle is a red glass tube, and I caress its coolness in my hands. This is my automobile. But this one's not a luxury vehicle. One of the old rubber wheels is stubborn and goes every direction but straight. This whacks my driving out of control. I follow Mama along the big windows, making a wavy trail across beige and brick-colored linoleum tiles.

At the front of the store, Mama peruses the vegetables, but continues past. "We're not getting vegetables today. We don't need them. Grandpa will give us plenty of lettuce and beans. And he'll have peaches soon." She thinks for a moment and shakes her head. "Apples won't be ready for another month."

"I wish we could get an orange."

"Yeah, honey, but there are no oranges now. They come in winter. You have to buy things when they're in season—that's how you can get them at a good price."

"But we don't buy lettuce and it's in season now, right?"

"Right. That's because Tha grows it in his garden and we don't need to buy it—just like we don't buy tomatoes, peppers, or peaches."

Mama stops next in front of the meat packages. The mounded paper packages of raw red meat rest on angled enamel shelves that hum. Mama's eyes move from one package to another. She reaches for a small one, but instead of putting the package in the chrome cart, she turns back the way she came. Mama raps on the white enamel double doors, and peers into the meat-cutting room. The rubber gasket-ringed windows are too high for me to see through. A white-capped, white-aproned man comes to the swinging doors and pushes one open toward us.

Mama holds out the cardboard tray of ground meat toward him. "Oh, could you make a smaller package for me?"

I hold my breath. What a brave thing to do! Most men—storekeepers, post office workers, cab drivers, bus drivers—are so mean that Mama and I try to avoid asking for anything.

The butcher man seems amused by the question…and nice. A man who is nice. "Sure. How much do you want? Half?" He raises his eyebrows.

Behind him, metal carts and enamel trays catch and reflect the strange bluish light of fluorescent lamps. Metal hooks dangle from the ceiling. But for the hooks, the room looks like an operating room in a hospital.

Mama nods. "Some soup bones, too?" she asks.

"Sure." The man slips back behind the enamel door.

"Mama! He wasn't mean."

"Yeah. Not like the butcher near your school."

From the back cooler, Mama chooses a cake of yeast and a half-dozen eggs. In the cooler I see thick glass bottles of milk, square and strong-necked. The colored paper caps on top tell what kind of milk is in the bottle, and in the middle of the accordion-folded paper is the cardboard disc with the dairy name. Mama saves the discs for pretend money, and we can use them to play tiddlywinks.

"There's a bottle of chocolate milk," I say, but Mama shakes her head.

"We're not going to buy fresh milk from the store. Uh-uh. You know the dairy delivers to our porch. We don't need to buy it here and carry the heavy bottles home."

We turn into the aisles.

"Are you going to get flour?"

Mama pauses to consider. "Yes. We're running low and we need to bake bread."

We pass by all the canned goods. Canned vegetables. Canned milk. Tuna. Canned tomatoes, tomato sauce, tomato paste. Canned juices. I stop in front of the juices and wait for Mama to say something.

"Can we get a can of juice?"

"It's too heavy. Remember we have to carry all of this. We have to wait until Dad drives to the Acme."

When Dad drives us to the supermarket two blocks beyond the A&P, we get big bags of potatoes, and a smaller one of onions, as well as soap bars, a bag of sugar, and cans of everything: juice, peas, spinach, evaporated milk. Mama uses that for her baking and her coffee. It's awful—like powdered milk, only warmer tasting and worse. I've asked her why she doesn't use bottled milk instead, and she always answers the same way. "Too expensive. Canned milk is good enough." She shakes her head in amazement. "It's all we had during the war you know. It's all we had. You get used to it."

At the end of the Acme shopping trip we get Green Stamps. We pay money for the groceries and the checker gives us little green stamps to put in little paper books. The pages are covered by crosshatched lines. On cold Saturday nights Mama pastes the stamps in with mucilage. She uses so much mucilage that the pages are stiff and shiny, but Mama doesn't want to risk losing a single stamp. Sometime she will take her green stamp books to the Green Stamp store on the far edge of downtown and choose a tool. In the catalog you can see the automatic washing machine you can get, or the color television set.

When I asked Mama about getting a washing machine or a TV, she just shook her head. "It takes too many stamps," she said.

"But what if Auntie gave us some for our book?"

"Even if Auntie donated all of her stamps, we wouldn't have enough books in a lifetime." Mama considers the possibilities. "Maybe we can get a hand-crank wall can-opener. Or a kitchen knife."

While Mama considers what else she really needs from the A&P, I lean on the red handle of the cart. Push forward, shift, push back. Forward towards tuna, shift and turn. I am a good driver. Maybe I'll drive a car someday. Maybe.

Mama doesn't know how to drive—none of the women in my family do, just like women don't smoke. The only women in our neighborhood who drive cars are teachers.

"Watch out!" gasps Mama, pulling my vehicle over to the side to let another shopper pass. Mama knits her eyebrows at me and takes the cart from my hands. She pushes it around to the next aisle, and I follow.

"Noodles?"

Mama shakes her head. "No. Grandma and I already made the egg noodles. They're up on the attic floor, drying."

At the end of the aisle are boxes of saltines. At school we have been learning about crackers—and practicing civil defense. We follow our teacher to the basement marked with a black and ochre sign that reads "CD."

"Civil defense," the teacher points out to us. "You must have a stock of canned goods, and a water jar." The teacher hands us crackers from a tin to taste. "Unsalted. Make sure you have *unsalted* crackers for your shelter at home," the teacher tells us. "You'll be too thirsty if you eat salted crackers in your shelter." The teachers don't tell us that this would come with the threat of a nuclear war, that everyone is on edge, and even they don't believe anyone could survive.

"Can we get some crackers?"

Mama looks up. "We have them at home."

"No, Mama, the unsalted kind. The teacher says we should get the unsalted ones for our shelter. Do we have a shelter?"

She shakes her head. "No. We eat the salted kind," she says firmly. "And no, we don't have a shelter."

"Why don't we?"

Mama lets out a sigh and pushes the cart forward. "I'll tell you when you're older," is all she says, not looking at me.

We turn the corner to the last aisle, to the baked goods. The black coffee grinder whines and screeches in the center of the aisle as an aproned man holds a paper bag to its silver spout. Brown powdered coffee clings to his apron, as messy as coal dust. I follow Mama with the cart, passing stands of coffee, coffee bags, and boxes of tea bags, then buns, breads, and cakes.

"What about that bread?" I point to the soft, sliced kind.

"Bread? Tch. We're not going to buy bread. We make our own."

Mama smiles and continues down the aisle to a rack at the end of the row. Here Mama selects a bag each of the hard rolls and soft buns. Mama leans down and whispers to me, "Day-old goods. Every bit as good as the fresh ones, just half the price."

She slips the bags into her basket. Across the aisle, near an enamel door, a baker in blue and white uniform watches, pretending she's not watching.

Mama keeps her back to the aisle and to the baker. There's a delicate dance of some kind going on. I'm unsure of the steps, so I just follow Mama as she moves on to the checkout.

"One bag or two?" the aproned man at the checkout asks Mama.

"Two." Mama smiles and nods toward me. She pushes the cart back to the windows.

"Did you ladies find everything all right?" Mama smiles and hands the man her coupons. The man rolls the top of the smaller bag shut and hands it to me.

"You help your Mama?" He asks. "That's a good girl," he says.

Mama places her pocketbook atop her groceries. "Come on," she says to me, lifting the large bag and swinging it onto her left hip. Out beneath the popcorn and sunshine sky, we climb back up the cindered hill. By the time we reach the top, my arms burn from carrying the weight of the groceries.

"I'm tired, Mama. Can we stop?"

Mama stands before me, her legs apart, feet planted firmly. The brown bag is seated comfortably on her hip. She looks at me. "You have to learn to carry," she says. "Use your hips!"

I try to put my bag against my body like Mama does, but the bag doesn't sit right. I cradle it to the side, but I still have to carry its weight with my arms.

Mama shakes her head and softly laughs. "You don't have hips yet. Someday you'll have hips to carry groceries on—and babies. That's what they're for." We cross the street to the cindered alleyways homeward.

Cornucopia

"Do you know what this is?" asks the teacher.

Hands go up. "Right! The Horn of Plenty. Today we're going to fill it in. Take out your crayons," says the teacher as she hands Nancy, the helper for today, a stack of mimeographed paper. The pale purple lines show a curled horn, an empty one. We hold the papers to our noses, sniff, and smile: fresh mimeo perfume.

"Now," says the teacher, "think of what foods come to us in autumn." Hands shoot up from all over the classroom.

Apples. Tomatoes. Pumpkins. Corn. Grapes.

"Draw," says the teacher.

And we do. Circles of purple and red, orange, and yellow spill aplenty.

On school windows, on grocery and five-and-dime windows, the Horn appears as part of a parade of autumn decorations celebrating the falling leaves, Halloween jack-o'-lanterns, and the black and white Pilgrims at Thanksgiving accompanied by turkeys displaying feather fans. Downtown, Horn of Plenty pictures appear in the huge display windows of Woolworth's in full color. Here in the picture, I see that the horn is a basket woven of golden straw. On one side the horn's narrow tip curls up and away, while its wide opening spills fruit and vegetables—apples, grapes, squash, corn, all the beautiful foods that can grow in a garden. All the colors contrast against gold, spilling out like a mountain stream.

I love the golden horn.

"Mama, where can we get one?"

"Get one what?" Mama continues pounding her heels

into the broad asphalt sidewalk. Her reflection in the store window shows that she's looking ahead, purposeful, her dark curls haloed by silver light against clouds.

"One of those." I hold her hand tightly and stand my ground, pointing to the Woolworth's plate glass windows.

"One of them?" Mama looks puzzled. "You mean that picture? We don't buy pictures."

"I know, Mama. Not a picture—one of those baskets with all the food. And pumpkins."

Mama's forehead wrinkles. "You want a Cornucopia?" She shakes her head. "That's just a picture, honey. It's a picture of the Horn of Plenty."

"It's real, Mama. The teacher…"

Mama shakes her head. "It's made up. It's a story."

"Why would people make it up?"

She sighs and then her eyes meet mine and hold them. "Oh honey, it's just art."

"But Grandpa has the Horn of Plenty. He has grapes and pumpkins and corn and peaches."

This stops Mama from speaking for a moment. She keeps walking, then says, "Tha has a green thumb," she says. "He grows things—tomatoes, beans, peppers, potatoes—he's even grown corn. He's tried everything."

Mama pauses and frowns. "You know that there's something wrong with that cornucopia picture. You can't have all those things at the same time. They're not all ready at the same time. Grapes and pumpkins…they're in different seasons."

"Oh."

I don't tell Mama that I don't believe her. I just know it's real. It has to be if we draw it at school and if all the stores have pictures of it. I want to find the magical horn that pours food and touch the weave of its golden straw—I want to hear the music of the fruits rolling out of the horn, pouring endlessly, continuously, so we can feast.

The Time of Anise

The black telephone on the black wire stand rings twice—two long rings, and then stops.

"That's Mom."

"Grandma?"

"Yeah. She wants us to come over now. Let's get ready."

Mama begins moving quickly through the kitchen, preparing the brown paper grocery bag, packing cutters, newly purchased bottles of red and green sugar, and her rolling pin.

"How did you know it was Grandma?"

"Because she rings twice."

"But you said we have one long ring on a party line…"

Mama pauses and looks at me. "On our party line, our signal is one long ring. Someone else has two short rings. And someone else has one short ring."

"Who does?"

"Well, we don't know…and it doesn't matter. We pick up for one long ring."

"But Grandma rings twice…"

"That's her signal to us. She rings twice, then stops."

"Oh."

Mama slips into the bag two folded aprons—one for her and one for me, though it's way too big for me. Last of all, she carefully places into the bag a small glass bottle of clear anise oil.

"Why did we have to buy anise oil, Mama? I want wintergreen. Grandma has some in her refrigerator. She used to make wintergreen candy. She told me so."

"We bought anise because Grandma makes anise cookies," Mama says firmly. "It's her tradition."

We've gone over this any number of times in the past few days. Anise is our flavor of the season and it's very good. But wintergreen. I love its cooling, buzzy taste. I love the name: wintergreen. I see a country Christmas card scene of perfect spruce trees covered in snow.

But there is no snow, at least not yet. In late November our hollow is cold, damp, and gray. It's time to bake cookies for Christmas and prepare for the dark time of year that we sweeten with cookies. We have just three weeks to mostly fill four five-gallon lard cans. The season of cookies begins at Grandma's house this day.

We put on wools: coats, scarves, hats, mittens. We pull on our rubber boots over our shoes, latch them, and set out under a watery gray sky. We've got to go three blocks to Grandma's house through the cinder-surfaced alleyways. Alleys are our roadways, Mama's and mine. They lead us to grocery stores, relatives, and the cemetery. They are the paths of our intimate landscape. Except for going to church or downtown in the bottom of the valley. For those trips, we dress up and use sidewalks.

When we walk slowly and roundabout to Grandma's we use the lower alley. It follows the creek past all the houses in Dutch Hollow. The lower alley is our summer road through blackberry patches and our autumn road to gather wild apples above the creek. Our winter road is the upper alley. Today we head uphill holding hands. Mama's outside arm cradles the bag, so light she doesn't even set it on her hip, and she walks. Near the top of the hill the sidewalk ends, and we turn onto the cindery surface of the alley.

Rains have left two lanes of puddles all down the alley where cars are driven; silver water mirrors reflect an overcast sky. It's almost cold enough for the puddles to freeze. Soon they'll be glass-capped with ice and all us kids will look for frozen air pockets to stomp and pop. Holding Mama's hand, I try to step into the sky mirror to make ripples in the reflected clouds, but Mama pulls me to the middle of the alley, trying to steer me out of temptation's way.

"Don't," she says. "You'll get your shoes and socks wet, and then what will we do?"

"We can put them on radiators."

"If you get wet, you'll get sick." Mama's lips make a straight line, showing how upset this makes her.

I know Mama worries about coughs and colds. She always wants me to stay warm and dry even though that couldn't have anything to do with the sicknesses in our valley. Smoke and burning coal are everywhere, and so is lung disease. Better to blame coughing on cold wet weather and damp feet.

We know nearly everyone's house along the alleyway. In them are our cousins, or cousins to our cousins, or just neighbors. In summer, the upper alley becomes a paradise for bicycles. All the neighborhood kids share their bikes with those of us who don't have any, and we know each parent's holler or whistle for bedtime. The upper alley is our path in October's time of trick-or-treat. At this time of year, though, the alley is empty except for Mama and me, and there's not a soul outside to holler hello to.

While we walk, Mama and I recite Grandma's cookie recipe, to see how much we remember.

"Like everything else, you start with the grease," Mama says.

"The grease?" I ask.

"Butter and lard, one pound each. Then you have to soften it."

"On the radiator."

"No! It would melt and then it wouldn't be any good. You put it near the radiator. Sugar is next—four cups. Cream the sugar in."

"Cream it?"

"Stir it in to get it mixed. Then come eggs. A half-dozen—six whole eggs. Beat them with a pint of milk. You mix the wet with the butter and sugar. Then you put the flour in, only a little at a time. Five pounds. A whole bag, but you have to put a little saleratus into the flour to make the cookies rise and then put in the anise. One whole tablespoonful. Then you chill it."

"And we can eat it!"

"No! Of course not!" Mama smiles and shakes her head. "It has raw egg in it…Oh, and we always make double the recipe. Two willow wash baskets full."

At the last block, we walk the path to grandma's yard. We climb the steps to Grandma's back porch and rush into the kitchen, leaving the gray day behind us. The kitchen is steamy and warm and smells of radiator. The silver beast beneath the window hisses its welcome. Lucky, Grandma's old black hound, lies at the far end of the room. He thumps his mangy tail and lifts only his eyes in welcome.

Mama sets her bag down on the table. Grandma's big maple cutting board and her red-handled rolling pin sit at one end of the table. Her bowls are waiting there too, a perfect nested set of six, from egg-cracking size all the way to the huge one that holds enough rising bread dough for four loaves. I love these bowls with their smooth milky white glass. They are bells without clappers, flowerpots without holes. The outside of each bowl is covered with red polka dots as big as the size of quarters. Polka dots! The name always makes me giggle. All over dark, navy blue rayon dresses, small white paint specks decorate all the women around: Grandma, her sisters and cousins, my mama... the dresses they wear at anniversaries, weddings—funerals, too—the bodices hold paper napkins stuffed inside for bursts of tears.

Grandma has already begun the dough before we arrive. The yellow dough waits for only one ingredient.

"I have the anise oil, Mom," Mama says. She removes cookie cutters and tools from the bag. Mama pushes up my sleeves and folds and ties an apron around me. Grandma finishes the dough and sets it out on the porch table covered with a damp dish towel.

"Grandma, why is the dough on the porch?"

"To cool it, honey."

"But why?"

"So you can roll it without it getting too soft."

"But you softened the butter…"

"…and lard," she pauses to consider. "You have to soften the butter and the lard so you can mix it with the other ingredients. Then, you cool it to get it firm. You bring it in a little at a time and let it warm (not too much) so you can roll it."

"It has to be just right," Mama adds. "If this rich dough gets too warm, it will melt and spread under the rolling pin. The cookies will bake without loft."

Grandma nods and I remember that the last cookies of the day are like this—too thin, flat, greasy, and too brown on the edges and bottoms.

Mama lays out the metal cookie cutters she has brought from our house: a star, a circle, a bell. Grandma's cutters of pearly gray metal nestle next to them: a tree, a star, and prettiest of all, a fluted heart and a fluted diamond for cutting ruffled edges in the dough. Each of Grandma's cutters has a punchout metal band for lifting the cutter of the dough, but the handles have gotten flattened by Grandma's big, strong hands pushing down a little too hard. All the cutters are too sharp for my hands and Mama and Grandma would just as soon keep me out of the path between the table and the oven. So, at the opposite corner of the table, farthest from the stove, Mama sets out red and green plastic cutters for me: a snowman, a Santa, and a tree. Though they press out pictures in the centers of the cookies, they don't cut anise cookies so well. They more mash the dough than cut it. Grandma gives me my own pile of dough and a tiny rolling pin with red handles like hers. She sets me on a chair where I can kneel and get to work until she needs me.

Grandma picks up her rolling pin. As she leans into the straight red handles, the bearings sing. In the gray light of spring, Mama and Grandma make noodles together on the enamel table, side by side, the red handles of Grandma's rolling pin firmly in her hands, gliding to a steady ball-bearing click. Mama's hands ride her solid maple rolling pin, the roots of her fingers bearing down; she extends her arms outward, never breaking contact with the handles. She lifts the pin and pounds the dough with a rumbling sound—a thundering.

But now, in this gray light of November, Grandma is the one who rolls and cuts dough while Mama manages the baking trays, slipping them in and out of the oven and gently lifting and sliding finished cookies into the waiting willow wash baskets. Carefully timed cookies will come out creamy, pale yellow. If Mama is lax, the cookies will bake to a crispy brown—the ones we'll eat first this season, dunking them in milk or coffee. The perfect pale cookies wait for company visits and polite nibbling.

My job is to place red or green sugar atop raw dough—a big responsibility, and it's painstaking work. The amount of sugar has to be just right. Too much sprinkle covers the beauty of the yellow dough. Too little leaves the cookies naked. There's the question of which colors are for which shapes. Hearts definitely get red. Diamonds do, too, so they look like the diamonds on playing cards. Stars and trees take green sprinkles, but bells need a little of both colors, carefully mixed. The trees need some green in the middle with red on the tips of their branches for ornaments. While decorating trees I slow a bit. I want them just right. Mama, wisps of hair straying from her hairpins and perspiration on her brow, looks at me pointedly and says, "Keep it simple, honey." Her eyes see a log jam of hundreds of cookies beginning to melt on trays.

We work quietly, smoothly, click and clatter. Grandma lovingly and firmly pushes the buttery dough into the smooth wooden board. Swirls of white flour swish over the yellow dough and now she pushes a shape down. Fluted diamonds, a tray of them. I watch her hands. Her big hands have swirling folds of wrinkles at the middle of her reddened fingers. One finger wears the wedding ring, red-gold, a tiny, clear, real diamond chip set in a gold heart. There was a grandpa once. He went away a long time ago and died before I ever knew him. Nowhere in Grandma's house is there a photo of him: the factory worker, the gandydancer, a tracklayer, the musician. Grandma still wears the ring, though. Red sugar falls from my hands and I want to press out diamonds, diamonds to make us rich and sparkle-filled.

In the kitchens of Mama's family far up the line, aunts are baking, too: dough pinwheels full of dates, chocolate-filled buttery leaf sandwiches, and small round balls of nuts and powdered sugar. Perfect cookies in clean and perfect kitchens.

Here this day we are warmed in the womb of this sagging kitchen rimmed in red, white, yellow. I look up. Red trims the yellowed stove clock. Red rims the small enamel pot, empty and resting on the stove. Red lids seal yellowed and rusting white tin cans bearing flour, sugar, salt. Red dots dance on white glass bowls of yellow cookie dough.

Trays of yellow cookie diamonds beneath my hands glitter with red sugar. Above the radiator, red-trimmed white curtains soften the silver-gray light outside the windows. Oven warmth and radiator glow wrap us like a quilt trimmed red against the chill outside.

At day's end, our legs ache from standing. Anise clings to our clothes, and even the dog smells like an anise cookie. We are wrapped in the warmth of anise on the cold walk home. In this holy time our incense is anise. We won't smell or taste it again until the holidays begin. When Christmas finally comes, the other side of the family will raise glasses of anisette. Grandpa, my Italian grandpa, will boom out, *Salud!*—a farewell to an old year and greeting to the new. The flavor and fragrance of anise will fill us until we eat the last of the pale yellow cookies and clean the crumbs from the tall tins on Valentine's Day, when we finish the last of the fluted hearts.

Relief Line

Dad sets the parking brake and takes papers from the dashboard. He stuffs them into the inside pocket of his coat. Mama helps me out of the car. We walk across cinders to a silent line of people. Our clothes are neither for every day nor fancy but are good enough for going downtown—which is where we are, except that Dad has driven behind all the downtown buildings and railyards.

"Why are we here, Mama?" I ask. I pull on her hand, but she doesn't look down to me.

"Hush," is all she says. Dad has a cigarette in one hand. He pulls the other across his thinning hair.

A long line of people snakes across a cinder lawn to a clapboard building. The building is like a house, but not as wide. Its dark windows have no curtains. I cannot understand what kind of house this is, or whom we are visiting. We join this line of dark-clothed adults, a river of wool coats stretching from the doors of the building, across its porch, down its stairs to the ground where we are. We are part of the silent stream and begin the long wait.

We are silent, but the air is saturated with the sounds of

coal cars rumbling past, metal bangs and screeches of coupling and uncoupling cars, humming and rattling like the garment factories—but so much grander and more frightening. We're near the railroad yards and shops but cannot see any trains. They are hidden by long rows of shop buildings. The loaded coal trains grind upgrade through the yards, through the cindered ground where we stand, through our bodies, and throb through our chests and heartbeats. It's like standing in line in church, where the sound waves from the pipe organ change our heartbeats as we move toward the altar for Communion.

The grinding locomotives fade away. I shake Mama's wrist to get her attention. "Mama?"

She leans down and whispers. "We're here to get Grandma's commodity food. Remember?"

Grandma gets free food sometimes because she's a poor person. We get it, too—from Grandma, and no one's supposed to know. Dad brings home the box of food to her and we divide it, most of it going to us. Grandma doesn't eat very much. Sometimes there isn't much food when Dad goes to get the box. They run out of things.

We wait for a long time for the line to move. For a while, Dad holds my hand, too, and I swing my arms, my parents' arms. I jump and squat. A fine misty rain fills the air and the line begins to move, haltingly.

"When can we go home?" I whisper upwards.

"We have to wait," says Mama quietly, no smile on her face. Drizzle begins, light but steady. Our collars go up and the line begins to move a little more smoothly. Dad heaves a sigh.

I pull down on Mama's hand, gently shaking her wrist. "Can we go home now?" I ask as quietly as I can.

Mama shakes her head. I'm not to ask more questions. We reach the porch steps. I grab onto the railing, ready to pull myself upward as soon as the line will allow. A step up, and another, and I can look under the rail at the line below. I see faces—still faces. I don't want to wear my coat or stand in line anymore. We're in line, though. We can't push off being here. Stand in line. Be quiet. Don't ask questions. It's the same at the polling station at the bottom of Grandma's street, where my parents cast votes. Keep quiet. Don't ask questions. Don't take any of those metal buttons that advertise whom we vote for.

It is our turn. We enter the wide and dark room. I can smell the creosote that covers the walls and makes them dark brown and shiny looking. It smells like school buildings, or railroad ties in summer. I look up, surprised to find the ceiling of the room isn't a ceiling at all. It's the inside of a roof, just like inside our attic, where flattened nails lie against boards, a red-brown stain shadowing each nail. The warped floorboards are like those in our attic, too—dry and dull. On this floor trails of curved hollows have been worn into the wood by footsteps. I wonder whose steps, for this isn't a place for anyone to live.

We face long wooden tables. Stacks of boxes and cans cover them. Mama whispers to me to be very quiet, and I am. Dad hands his papers to a woman neatly dressed in a navy-blue suit. She doesn't smile. She takes the papers and directs Dad down the table. He takes a cardboard box and fills it: a box from this stack, that stack. Rectangular boxes, a cylindrical box, a small thick one. Several sizes of folded brown paper bags slump in rows. Their pointed corners bend toward each other at the top like a gift, but without bows. All the cardboard and paper are the same color: a deep golden brown—the color of Dad's wool army blankets he has kept from the war he fought in. We follow Dad to another table holding silver cans—some small, some rectangular with rounded corners, and some large ones with indented ring bands around them like tomato juice cans at the Acme—but none of the cans have pictures or colored paper labels. All the packages and cans have the same bold, black letters: "U" and "S."

I point to the letters and ask, "Mama, what does that say?"

"Shh," she whispers. "U.S. Government."

Dad moves to the food boxes on the far end of the room and takes one box, the shape of the butter box in the grocery store, like the waxy boxes of yellow and white. This one, though brown, looks just like them. Butter! Maybe we'll have butter! On Sunday nights Dad spreads white oleomargarine on crackers and saltines for a special treat. But to taste real butter on saltines…I look up at Mama and smile and tug on her hand, but all she says is "hush" and holds my hand firmly.

Dad lifts his filled box and turns. Mama and I follow down the length of the building and out a side door. Out in the drizzle, a line of people with papers still crosses the cindered yard. We head out away from it, relieved to get to our car with the box.

At afternoon's end, in pouring rain, we arrive at Grandma's house. As we unload the car I look again at the brown boxes and the strange tin cans with their black letters.

"Mama, where are the pictures?"

"Pictures?"

"The food pictures on the cans."

"You mean the paper labels?"

"Yeah, Mama, the pictures with the colors of food—like green peas and yellow creamed corn."

"No pictures here, sweetheart," answers Dad. He smiles a strange smile. "Just plain black words."

"Why words?"

"Because they're not selling it to you. They're giving it to you."

"It's *free*?"

Dad looks at me and pauses. He inhales, looks away, and doesn't say anything more.

In Grandma's house, we divide up the commodities: a sack of flour, and one of sugar. Oats, cornmeal, lard, canned meats. Butter, too! What a luxury! Then Mama opens a very long and narrow rectangular box holding something wrapped in cellophane. It looks like clay—but bright orange. I've never seen anything quite like it before.

"Here," she says. She slices a square from the end of the orange block and holds it out to me with a smile. "It's cheese, honey. Cheddar."

Smooth and salty, the cheddar fills my mouth with pleasure. I bite again and again, making crescent cutaways on the slice until only a corner remains.

Candles

Mama and I climb up our hill from the hollow, dress shoes slapping and clacking against slate sidewalks until we reach the top and begin our descent down, down, down to the valley, to the German Catholic church that blesses our babies and our dead. Our light-colored hats are firmly pinned on our heads as we careen, and our stockinged feet slide in our pointed shoes, jamming our toes. The valley's steepness pulls us as we hold on to each other's white-gloved hands and our white purses.

At the bottom, we hurry. Mama pulls me across the asphalt flatness of each cross street to the safety of the curbs. Her dark curls bounce.

"Why are we walking so fast?"

"We'll be late. We can't be late for Mass."

To the north, the high-pitched Irish bells of Nativity Parish call the neighborhood to Mass, while to the south, the large Polish bells, the high-towered bells of St. Stanislaus beckon. Small Protestant church bells ring in between, but for us, they don't count. The nuns tell us that because those people aren't Catholic, it doesn't matter what they do.

At the bottom of the mountainside we can see our

church's crowd flocking in those last two city blocks. Here
my mother's hand tenses, her shortened arm stiffer than
usual. We have one stoplight crossing before reaching the
church's brick parish holdings. We pass the stone Protestant church that borders our church's rectory. The doors
are open, and their service is letting out. The people are
smiling as they come down the steps. I try to peek inside.

"Do Protestants believe in Jesus too?"

"Well, yes, but…it's not the same."

"Sister says I can't play with Protestants at school. She
says Protestants might invite me into their church. Mama,
why can't I go inside a Protestant church?"

"That's a mortal sin."

"A mortal sin?"

"It means it's a big sin. You can't go to heaven if you
commit a mortal sin…like murder."

We race through the alleyways between buildings and
onto the asphalt stretch around our church's brick school.
Now the deep bell of our church sounds in paired rings:
only four times. We rush to the vestibule at the far end
of the church, for we wouldn't dare go into the side of
the nave this late and make such a bold entrance as Mass
begins. We pull the heavy doors of the back of the church
open and enter the soft yellow light of the marbled vestibule. We pass rows of red glass holding white wax candles,
hundreds of them, displayed on tiered black iron frames.
They are bright with flames.

I tug on Mama's hand as we hurry past. "Can we light
a candle?"

"Maybe after Mass."

We dip our fingers in the marble holy water font, cross ourselves, and drip past the wary eyes of the ushers as we make our way to the back of the church.

Mama makes a quick decision. She gestures for me to climb the back stairs to the loft. The organ pews are where music rumbles belly and jaws—much better than the on-time pews midway in the large nave. At this height, we are almost level with the top of each tall stained-glass window. It's a grand place to be. Painted angels float above the alcoves of each window and saints stand in between. In the lower part of the church, the stained-glass windows are good company for me, putting colored lights on my skin, but up here I can talk to the angels and saints lining the ceiling and rumble with the organ's bellowing blasts.

Chimes ring. The introit begins from the front of the church. We stand. Chants ring and music rumbles and the mumbled responses rise to us in the loft. The Mass is in Latin. The nuns know the Latin, but our family does not.

Up and down we go from kneelers to seats, standing again with toes snug beneath the padded wooden kneeler. Down we go, heads hung. We rise and fall. Each time we stand our clothes sound like wind and waves as we ready to sing or call the responses. But each time we sit to listen, we hear coughing and wheezing. Ladies' hats bob brightly in springtime colors: cream, pastel blue, yellow, and white with matching netting. Mama's is a tasteful cream. At home and around the neighborhood, Mama wears babushkas, but for church, Mama wears a hat. The netting makes diamonds on her face in the color-filtered light. Below in the nave, there are mostly women's hats because there are fewer men—especially old men.

The waves settle for the priest's homily. His words are droned. We drift through the solo lost in light and shadow, coal-saturated air, and rising dust motes. Chanting floats in the air. Reedy chords of the pipe organ swell until the final notes sweep us outdoors.

After Mass, Mama and I wait until the church is nearly empty before descending into the vestibule. The candles in the rack glow in the hush of the empty room.

"There are a lot of candles lit, Mama!"

"Yeah. Lots of people making prayers. Oh," she pauses. "Look, there aren't any for us here. They're all lit. Let's go to the candles at the front of the church."

We move quietly to the pews near the altar and slide into one up front where we can see the candles. Nearby, nuns and parishioners kneel, rosaries in hand. It's so much quieter without all the people coughing.

Mama and I huddle and whisper.

"Why do people light the red glass candles and not the candles at the altar?"

"The candles at the altar are for Mass. The candles in the red glass are the ones for our prayers—the ones we light to ask for favors."

"What kind of favors?

"A wish. When you say a prayer, you make a wish. If someone is sick, you pray for her to get better. Or if someone is far away, that they'll come home okay.

Mama reaches into her purse. "I have to find a coin… here. Now think about what you want to pray for."

Mama walks quietly to the altar rail. I follow. Our footsteps echo through the large church. The old women up front don't seem to notice us—they stay bent over their rosaries. The nuns watch us, though, and smile.

Mama puts the dime in the slot. It rings out over the hushed church. Mama pulls a narrow wooden stick from the sand at the side of the rack.

In the rows of red glass, flames waver, each with a personality: some straight and clear, some unsure, some sputtering, or flapping. On the far sides of the rack, much larger candles stand like sentinels in tall red glass.

"Please can we light one of those tall ones?"

"No, no. Those are dollar candles. We can't spend that much."

Mama puts her hand over mine, guiding the stick to a candle with a strong flame. We bring the flame to an unlit candle on the lowest tier, holding it carefully until it catches. Mama blows out the stick and guides my hand to the container of sand at the side of the candle rack. Together we twirl the stick in the sand, and I drink in the delicious smell of the punk smoke. Mama leads me back to a pew.

We kneel. "Now you can say a prayer for someone. Who do you want to pray for?" Mama whispers to me.

I think about Grandpa, Zi' Ming, Grandma. "Um, Grandma. She seems sad."

Together Mama and I watch the candle for a few moments then Mama takes my hand. As I leave the church, I see our candle and its small, strong flame. I hope it will stay lit a long time.

II. Composing the Landscape: Trains

Like his contemporaries in the Hudson River School art movement, George Inness composed a landscape and created an experience. In *The Lackawanna Valley*, Inness painted a landscape so captivating it is as if you've arrived at a portal to the place. As intended in this style of painting, your eyes move back and forth, farther and farther into the painting, to resolve the asymmetry of objects: from locomotive to tree and boy, across and back farther to the roundhouse, then across to church spire, until finally your eyes reach the mountains and are drawn up to the sky. Half of the painting is sky—an immensity of room in which to dream—but it cannot hold you. Your eyes drop back down into the foreground of the painting so you can repeat the experience if you wish. Inness's landscape is one to linger in.

In truth, instead of depicting or composing a landscape, Inness *contrived* a landscape. The painting, *The Lackawanna Valley,* was an advertisement. George D. Phelps, the first president of the Delaware, Lackawanna & Western Railroad, commissioned the painting from Inness in 1855 for seventy-five dollars. Inness desperately needed the commission to support his family. He wrote to his wife, Lizzie, who was left behind in New Jersey:

Scranton, September 1855

My dearest wife:

Above all the things in the world I would love to see you. I have to think of you the more that I am in trouble. I left my baggage at St. John's and walked to Stroudsburg. The scamp never sent it. I left for Scranton with the promise from the stage propri-etor that it should be sent to me the next day. It has not come, and I shall now be at expense to get it. I had to buy a shirt and other things, so that my money is almost gone. Send me ten dollars. I fear I shall need it. You will have to wait until I can send you money or until I return. There is no other way.

I kiss you a thousand times, my Love, and will has-ten to you as soon as possible. Kiss my little ones for me. I will write you a long letter soon.

Your affectionate husband,
George Inness

Phelps wanted Inness to prominently feature his railroad and new brick roundhouse in the painting. He wanted many tracks shown, whether they had been laid on the ground or not. Inness refused, unwilling to advertise what did not exist. Phelps demanded not one, but *four* locomotives placed in the scene. Again, Inness refused, but relented and painted four locomotives: one straining on the grade in the painting's foreground, and three others at work near the roundhouse farther back in the painting. Inness used his artistic talent to foreshorten the view. He placed all the focus on the locomotive leaving the valley and painted the lettering Phelps demanded: DL&WRR—Delaware, Lack-awanna and Western Railroad—prominently on it. And in subversive protest, it is said, Inness painted the central, prominent locomotive without an engineer.

Inness's *Lackawanna Valley* captures the moment when all the necessary elements of iron and coal, railroads, and fledgling city came together to blossom into the Industrial Revolution in North America.

The Stourbridge Lion was the first railroad steam loco-motive to be operated in the United States. It was brought over from Great Britain in 1829 and ran in Honesdale, east of the Lackawanna Valley. The locomotive was too heavy for the rails on which it ran, and so it was never used for its intended purpose of hauling coal.

The development of the DL&W Railroad was inter-twined with the fortunes of the Scranton brothers, for they had founded the railroad to transport iron and coal prod-ucts from the Lackawanna Valley. In the 1840s, Selden T. and George W. Scranton chose the Lackawanna Valley as the site for a series of rolling mills. Basing their financ-ing on the belief that Slocum Hollow contained high-grade iron ore, limestone, and the coal needed for blast furnaces, the Scranton family created the Lackawanna Steel Com-pany—the largest in the country. To their dismay, the local iron ore turned out to be low-grade, and limestone had to be hauled into the valley—a difficult task over the steep mountains. This was done using a gravity railroad, hauling raw materials up to stationed planes and allowing the cars to move by gravity down the other side. The valley's enormous deposits of anthracite coal proved to be the best possible resource for solving their dilemma—it made a new form of transportation possible.

In the early nineteenth century, smelting iron with anthracite was new, as were railroads to transport manufactured goods. By choosing to manufacture T rails for the nation's rapidly developing railroads, the Scrantons created a highly successful operation. Lackawanna Iron's mills freed the railroads in the United States from having to import rails from Britain. This, in turn, encouraged the expansion of railroads to build the American landscape throughout the nineteenth century. Anthracite was crucial in the rise of metal manufacturing and steam power, and it offered a new source of heat. At the same time anthracite was pulled from the ground, railroads pushed out of the steep Lackawanna Valley and provided energy and power for motion never before seen.

The Lackawanna Valley captures the very moment of a great transition in the world: the marriage of anthracite mining and the production of iron rails. George Inness composed well, balancing the industrial revolution and natural landscape at the moment before the balance was tipped, with a straw-hatted, cow-herding boy as fulcrum, viewing it all in wonder.

Though I cannot pinpoint the start of my relationship with Inness's painting, I know it has always been there, and I was born into it just as I was born into a relationship with my parents. The Inness painting haunted my childhood in the 1960s. I was captivated by it because I recognized it. Warmth spread in my middle. It was familiar—it was home. The shapes of rounded blue mountains set against pink haze—these mountains were blue bosoms, as comforting to me as burying my face in my mama's apron, the scent of her, looking up to her soft rounded chest.

Yet, I was intrigued with the unfamiliar in Inness's *The Lackawanna Valley*—the small, woodburning, steam locomotive bedecked with funnel-shaped smokestack and painted wooden cowcatcher. I imagined it in motion, working its way upward on a curve, crossing a stream or river, leaving behind a settlement—what would someday become my home place, the city of Scranton.

This is not at all the landscape I saw in my childhood. One hundred years after the creation of George Inness's painting depicting our valley, the diesel locomotives of five railroads corralled us into the distinct neighborhoods of our city. Coal trains pulsed through our sleep, their engines grinding and growling.

Each hillside was terraced into yards bearing closely stacked wooden houses. Beneath the streets, unseen hands mined and withdrew coal for fuel, lining our roads and railroads with spilled black diamonds. Coal hummed its black song through everything we did. Sometimes the ground beneath us spouted smoke from minefires or collapsed completely. Ours was an ashen landscape veiled by gray air.

The valley was a separate world from the mountaintops. Throughout my growing up, those of us living in the Lackawanna Valley touted ourselves as the proud dwellers of the largest and best coal valley in the world. We didn't

know or didn't want to acknowledge, halfway through the
20th century, that our valley's wealth had peaked in 1901,
when Lackawanna Iron departed for Buffalo, New York,
and had been diminishing ever since. We didn't know that
after the 1960s it would all be gone: no more mines, rails,
tall buildings, or the DL&W railroad's signature passenger
train, the *Route of the Phoebe Snow*.

The Lackawanna Valley of the painting was a mythical
place. A contrivance: not a reality. And strangely, although
we lived in that same valley, I didn't connect the painting
to the river. A *valley* means there is a *river*. Which river?
I always wondered as a child. The Lackawanna River did
not exist for us. It was not what we thought of when we
said the word *river*. We didn't mention those waters except
in joking. It ran with sewage and coal mine tailings from
all the little towns built along it, all the way down through
our city's downtown, a ribbon of orange suffused with *yellow boy*, the slang name for sulfuric acid.

Orange waters lapping against blackened banks lined
with coal: that's what I remember. Almost as if it were
shameful to have our city built along such a deteriorated
waterway, those of us living in the Lackawanna Valley
tried not to think about it much. We surely would not
have brought visitors to the river's banks to take a look.
We would have, instead, brought our visitors up along
the highway that snaked eastward out of the valley, Route
307. And just before crossing the eastern ridge and leaving the valley entirely, we'd have invited our visitors to
pull over at a Works Project Administration (WPA) overlook, proudly built by unemployed men (my dad included)
during the Great Depression. We'd have shown them the

valley and downtown from a distance, where the mists appeared pleasant.

If I had been able to paint the landscape of my valley and the city of my childhood, I would have composed it this way: everywhere grimy black with coal and obscured in a smoky haze while coal trains run over and under, around and through, like a continuous black thread.

Trains

We feel them all day, all night. Coal trains, impossibly long, call us from our dreams, or whatever we are doing, to listen and to look for them. We are swept into the story of trains, and we are told that this is the way it should be, as good as it can be, these trains moving coal. Who would we be without coal? The answer sounds like what the Cowardly Lion says in *The Wizard of Oz*: "Nuttin'. Nobody." Coal and rails make us who we are.

I didn't get to see a steam locomotive. I was born too late for that. The very last coal-burning locomotives of the DL&W were melted down for scrap right around the time I was born. But the pictures of them are still everywhere. Steam engines race through our Alice and Jerry first-grade readers, and the teacher's wooden alphabet stamper set has a steam locomotive—the largest stamper in the wooden case. It is magnificent.

The real trains outdoors, the squarish diesel locomotives pulling their coal cars, don't chug like in "The Little Red Caboose" song. They have no column of smoke and no long wail of a steam whistle. The diesels steal past. Mama and I have to contend with them day and night in our hollow and everywhere we go. Under, over, around, and through, Mama and I weave among trains and steel tracks and coal placed everywhere. Trains separate us from our relatives on the mountain. They run below the park across the gorge, and past the pool and the cemetery at the edge of our own neighborhood. They rumble in the tunnel beneath the street of my elementary school, pass our yards filled with laundry, trestle over streets. The trains of five railroads ring our city's downtown, and the sounds of their horns are so much a part of our valley that the high school students downtown are taught to memorize the horns of the locomotives of each of the different railroads to learn musical intervals and chords.

Mama and I walk all the streets and alleyways of our neighborhood, and we can go many different routes to downtown and across the gorge to the park, but even though we cross paths with trains everywhere, we can't follow them. Trains are quick and mysterious. They know something we don't.

◆ ◆ ◆

"Count them," my parents tell me whenever we see a string of coal cars or boxcars. That's the way we practice numbers. So I begin. It's hard to count the gondola cars of a coal train. They all look exactly the same. I can't move my eyes away from them for a second as they pass the flashing guards.

"Can you count to 100?" Dad asks.

I don't answer so that I don't lose track. "99, 100, 101, 102…109, Dad! It has 109 cars!"

"That's a mile-long coal train."

♦ ♦ ♦

Passenger trains, with their sleek and lovely, round-nosed locomotives come through downtown and up the gorge, but never in our neighborhood. They can never see us hidden in our little hollow, playing king of the hill on a dirt pile, our laundry strung the length of our yards, clean underwear and rags hidden on the inner lines so the neighbors won't see them. But the L-shaped switching engines pass close to us and carry freight and coal from the collieries down the line. They ring the mountain above our houses. Long before horns and bells tell us the train has reached the mountain road crossing, we hear the locomotive coming all the way up the hollow. Above its growling, the engine hisses its song of stops and starts: *da da dad a DUMM CHuhhhh da da dad a DUMMM…*and we hear the string of boxcars or gondola cars drawn through our hollow like a strange wind.

We watch lots of gondola cars. We get up close enough to see the black iron beads of rivets along the iron ribs and black iron couplers. The couplers look like the plastic ones on toy Lionel trains, but these are black and powerful iron claws clasping one to another to another.

Mostly the freight cars roll smoothly, but sometimes one boxcar sways more violently, rocking and tilting, screeching a protest with its wheels, as if it doesn't want to go on this ride out of the valley. "We are going to go anyway," says the train. The metal hands of the couplers hold the protesting car at either end. "We are going to go anyway," say the cars on either side of the errant boxcar. That boxcar is like a small child being pulled by two parents, pulled down the road, pulled on a journey she doesn't want to go on. Maybe the car will pull away. Maybe this time it will jump the track.

We tell trains apart by their colors and symbols like we do for baseball teams, and I know them all. One kind of locomotive is red and has the symbol of a diamond on a white flag. Another is red with a white liberty statue. There's a blue one with a blue shield on its yellow nose. The kind that rides through our hollow is gray with a nose of yellow and a ribbon of brown on its side. That's a DL&W and it's the kind that has the largest and fanciest passenger train station downtown. It stands like a gray fortress above the Roaring Brook, walling the downtown off from the rest of the city. Mama loves to visit the passenger station and see the trains there.

Sometimes we stand in front of the station to catch a bus home, and all of a sudden Mama will need to run and see a passenger train leave, taking me with her.

"Oh! There's a train coming! You want to go see?" Mama asks me. We are on Lackawanna Avenue. It's not really a question. "Of course you do," Mama answers herself, her grip on my small hand tightening.

Mama's steps quicken. She tilts her head upward with a smile. I want to say: *No, Mama, I don't want to go there. I don't want to stand next to the tracks while the train roars and hurts my ears. No, Mama!* But we are running and out of breath, and she is still pulling my arm forward. She makes my small legs run to her hastening strides.

We dash across the broad avenue to the rough, wide cement stairs that lead up to the tracks. We hurry up the

steps, her leather heels tapping a rhythm out of sync with
the approaching train. "Come on!" she says, breaking into
a run along the tracks, and we enter beneath a canopy of
translucent windows that echo the shape of a passenger
train. The windows of the platform canopy alter the light,
coloring it smoky gold, giving the sense of entering a
cathedral. But now, with a train coming, the platform with
its glass ceiling becomes a concert hallway, magnifying
the rumbling, and we are swept into it. We rush beneath
pillars and arches of iron speckled with rivets that hold up
the glass canopy, draping over us like some tropical trees
hammered out of a blacksmith's dream.

We are now next to the gray stone station, an altar or
a castle five stories high. Inside, the walls and floors are
made of marble and the ceiling is made of stained glass—
so full of rich things, it's a palace. We can't see that now
from the platform as we run. And we're still running when
the yellow nose of the lead locomotive overtakes us,
thrumming, roaring, slowing to a deep-voiced metal halt
just beyond the station doors.

"It's going to New York, this train," says Mama, still
panting. Gray cars, ribboned with maroon stripes beneath
the windows, gold-yellow lettering. Up above us, behind
the rectangular glass windows, the passenger car suspends
the men in suits, the women in all colors of hats. Some
sit comfortably, reading newspapers, not noticing us at all
while others stare straight ahead.

Mama rushes along the cement platform pulling my
hand so that my arm is outstretched to meet hers. She pulls
harder, panting and smiling as if this is the train she'll be
boarding and she's just made it to the platform on time.

At my level I can see the gray flannel pant legs of the suited men and the skirt lengths of the ladies lining up to board the train. They join the other passengers seated at the windows, not looking down at us. Trackside, at my level I can see the trucks of the trains—those great oiled sets of wheels, interlaced with hoses. Steam is coming out from them and I don't want to get close: steam burns. And the size of those wheels...the height of those cars...dizzying. Dangerous. They could crush us.

Over the thrumming of the waiting train, blurry, undecipherable words come from loudspeakers mounted on the station. Mama points to a uniformed man with glasses next to the train. His flat, dark blue wool hat is just like the one my dad wears for his dress firefighter uniform.

Mama leans down close and says in a loud whisper, "Now watch that man. That's the conductor. He's going to signal the train to go. Watch now, it's going to leave." For a moment I freeze, and begin to back away from the train. The rumbling starts again.

Mama is holding me in place and leaning down to me. "Do you want to wave goodbye?" she says with a smile on her face.

We are too close, Mama. The steam will burn us—can't you see? The train will sweep us away in its rumble and wind!

The rumbling rises, coming in deafening waves. My heart beats wildly—my heart tries to beat its own rhythm, but this close to the train, sound waves crash over and through us.

Then the train begins to move. I cannot breathe or

speak. I become vessel, a fleshy drum in tune with the train. Mama holds my hand, but the locomotive sweeps me up into its immense, dark heart, pushing up and out of the valley. I try to hold on, sobbing, but a piece of my heart tears and is taken away.

◆ ◆ ◆

Icy rain strikes the windowpanes of my bedroom. I pray for snow. Attached to my window is the paper Santa the National Bank gave me. He is so jolly and perfect, his face rosy against the watery gray light outside. His green-mittened hand is raised in salute. At his feet rests a brown cloth sack brimming with wrapped gifts. Every day I greet him, leaning on the bedroom windowsill to talk with him. "I'm glad you're coming," I tell him. When I say that I want a doll dressed in an old-fashioned wool cape with a hat and a train, he doesn't tell me I need to ask for clothes. He accepts what I say, cheerily. We'll keep each other good company until Christmas Eve, when Mama and I put ornaments on the tree in the parlor.

One snowy day it's time for Mama and me to begin our holiday shopping and visit the store Santa. Avoiding slippery sidewalks, we make our way down the steep mile to the valley bottom. At the last avenue, Cedar, we cross the bridge over the wide Roaring Brook, passing the buried remains of enormous furnaces that melted steel, manufactured rails, and created our city. We follow the sidewalk to the massive black trestles full of tracks beneath which we must cross. If the nearby train station is a cathedral or a castle, we are about to enter the side gates of the kingdom as we cross waters and pass beneath towers and bridges. But sometimes I wonder, if the train station is a castle, who is King? It can't be a diesel locomotive. That's too modern. It must've been a steam locomotive. Or coal. Coal is King, and the trains are servants in armor.

The railroad shops and main railyards loom above us. Though we hear the slamming of boxcars and screeching, we can't see any trains. They are hidden from view. What we see before us is a trestle of iron blackness suspended over the street leading uphill to downtown—black iron, blacker than any coal, spanning the sky.

We approach the broadest trestle as if entering a tunnel. We keep a steady pace on the greasy sidewalk and walk boldly beneath it, but I feel Mama's hand tense. Daylight and the snow-lined sidewalks turn to darkness. We breathe in creosote. Above us, suspended like sooty stalactites, black dirt icicles hang from the trestles—they are there even in summer's heat.

Mama and I continue forward without speaking—we wouldn't be able to hear each other anyway, over the traffic echoing beside us. We can finally see the sky again, and we head uphill to broad Lackawanna Avenue. We breathe a sigh of relief. Above us, the sky is filled with electric lines swaying in the wind, and yellow traffic lights swing back and forth. We cross quickly, in front of many angry cars with chrome-gleaming grill teeth bearing down on us— impatient beasts that can strike. Mama and I jump to the safety of a flagstone curb and turn onto the asphalt side-walk. Behind us, along the avenue, old and young men stand wearing wool coats and hungry eyes. They are lined up along the vacant-windowed buildings and dirty store-fronts that lean against the railyards. They are all cough-ing, and they lean over to spit on the sidewalk. "Don't look at them," Mama tells me.

Mama and I put our heads down and continue down the avenue parallel to the empty buildings and men. Grit from the sidewalks swirls up into the air. "On windy days like this we used to get cinders in our eyes," Mama reminds me, "and on our legs."

I nod. She always tells me this when we walk Lacka-wanna Avenue on a windy day. She was younger when the coal-burning locomotives were thick on the tracks beside the avenue and encircled the whole downtown. Though I wouldn't want cinders in my eyes or cinders to scratch my legs under her full-skirted dresses in summer, I wish for the steam locomotives whenever I hear that wistfulness in Mama's voice.

There are no huffing locomotives now, though there is still smoke filling the valley from the burning culm dumps and minefires beneath our streets and yards. Sparks no lon-ger come from streetcar lines, but from the sparking hol-iday lights and artificial green garlands strung overhead and woven onto black lampposts. The holiday garlands are the only green against gray skies and the landscape of dark buildings in all shades and hues of gray to black.

As we walk down the avenue, away from the trestles and the big DL&W train station, we move toward a world of women, children, and families: clean glass windows filled with color, stores warmly lit from within, and gifts we can wish for.

"Let's go to Woolworth's first," Mama suggests.

"Mama, can we get a treat there?"

"Maybe. Later."

"Can we look at toys?"

"Yes. Today we'll look at toys. Let's look here. Think about what you'd like for Christmas so we can tell Santa."

Mama and I head to the doors beneath the red and gold sign. For us there is always a sense of pride in coming to the store, because this Woolworth's was the first one like it in the country. Woolworth's is the store where we can look and talk to our hearts' content because no salesperson will follow us around trying to help us and making Mama nervous because we can't afford to buy in those stores. Woolworth's is friendlier because we are on our own.

We pass the photomat near the entry and walk along the stools of the lunch counter that run the length of the store. The counter is half full, mostly men in rumpled suits looking down at the thick-walled railroad-ware cups in front of them. The waitress looks tired. She leans on the counter between the big square glass juice fountains. Her hair is just like that of all the women in my neighborhood—pulled back away from her face with a froth of curls in front—a style from the 1940s. Just like Mama's hair.

A little sign propped on the counter displays pictures of turkey sandwiches piled high in layers, with lettuce between creamy beige bread slices. A toothpick holds it tight. Mama wouldn't ever let me have one. "Turkey that far out of season? No," she always says.

Usually, we stop at Woolworth's when we have time between buses, and we look at everything on the main floor—from parakeets to penny candies shaped and colored for each holiday of the year. But for toys at holiday time, we go straight to the wide stairs that lead to the toy department in the basement.

Mama and I walk through the aisles and aisles of model cars and planes, and then to the aisles of dolls. We look at them in their cellophane windowed boxes.

Some have beautiful lacy clothes, and some can talk if we pull a string.

"Look." Mama points to shelves of unboxed dolls that have folk costumes from around the world. "Wouldn't it be nice to have one of these?"

I don't answer Mama. I mostly want to go to the aisle of Lionel trains.

Lionel trains travel their circuits in the living room or parlor of every relative's house at Christmastime (except for Grandma's). Every one of my uncles has a platform supposedly for his kids, although there is something about the way the uncles' grins freeze as they push the black lever on the transformer—they look as if they have left the room and are somewhere far away. I have one uncle who is so up-to-date with each new appliance in his house that he has a color television set in his living room, and it draws all the attention. But at Christmastime, the color television set is forgotten. His toy train platform takes up most of the room—the fanciest one any of us has ever seen, complete with papier-mâché tunnels, working crossing guards, and water towers with bubbling water. I love the model steam locomotive—a manageable-sized locomotive for me to get close to. I love watching it go round and round on the trestled, figure-eight track layout, disappearing into tunnels and coming out again. I love the tiny crossing guards dutifully protecting miniature round-roofed cars. It's all so perfect on its green and gray painted platform landscape. The only detail that uncle missed on his train platform was the burning culm dumps with their haloes of smoke and their blue flames at night.

"Mama, I want to see the trains."

Mama sighs. "Okay."

We go into the aisle stacked with orange and blue boxes of Lionel trains. A few of the boxes have windows showing special gondola cars and towers. Mostly though, I can't see anything but the name "Lionel" on the boxes. I walk past them and puzzle. What's in those boxes? They are mysterious. Secretive. Toys for boys only, and their dads. Hidden machinery, row upon row. It's like the railroad yards: rows upon rows upon rows of tracks—a place we cross beneath but can never see. A secret world. The yard sends out clangs and vibrations through the ground and through our bodies. I hear the boxcars being slammed around. I see the coal cars entering the yard behind the buildings and coming out the other side. But what really happens in the train yards? No one explains it or what's inside the Lionel boxes either.

I take my time, looking and concentrating. It would be so lovely to have a train and a little town of my own. I wish I could have my own set for a platform. I decide to give it a try.

"Mama, could I have a train?"

"What? You're a girl!"

"But I like them!"

"Oh *phh*…" Mama swats her hand in the air. "You don't need that. It has electricity. You have dolls." She says this to me the same way she says girls can't play baseball.

"But Mama…" I begin to protest. With a *tch* she shakes her head, then takes my hand.

Mama and I head farther down the avenue to the department stores that define the center of downtown. Both around the corner and across the street, green caterpillar buses line the curbsides four at a time, waiting patiently for passengers. Women with wool babushkas and men with fedoras and cigarettes huddle against the building beneath the canopies, some resting their paper shopping bags on their feet to keep them dry. Over the sticky whoosh of tires on wet pavement, a Salvation Army worker keeps her bell steadily ringing as she stands beside her red kettle.

Mama and I slip through the sidewalk crowds and push the revolving doors inward to join the shoppers in the store. We waddle through the glass doors, jostling among shoppers with their paper bags. Mama and I usually shop in the bargain basement where kids' shirts, dresses, pants, and even underwear are set out on square tables for everybody to see. It's the worst place in late summer. That's when lots of mamas bring their kids to buy clothes for school. Sometimes the moms snatch clothes from the tables so other moms don't get them. Sometimes we find just the right shirt or dress, but it's the wrong size, and someone else has just gotten the last one. Today though, Mama and I head to the escalator in the center of the store. Mama quickly pulls me onto the silvery step. Holding tightly to her hand, I turn back to see the stations of goods—wallets, suitcases, freshly made candies, record albums, men's hats, ladies' gloves, umbrellas, perfumes, cosmetics. Small crowds of customers in dark wool coats encircle each station like ants. Rising above them, we hear the murmurs of the shoppers punctuated by the store's mysterious paging bell. We spiral up and up through several sets of escalators until we reach the toy floor. We pass aisles of dolls and stuffed animals and head straight to the corner where Santa or Santa's Helper sits on a throne.

"Do you want to see Santa?" Mama asks me.

"Yes, Mama," I answer confidently.

We join a line of mothers and children that reaches back to the toy aisles. One small boy bursts out crying just as he reaches the throne and is quickly led back to his mother. We all stare in surprise as his mother drags him away.

"Why is he crying, Mama?" I whisper upwards.

"I guess he's just too little to know what's going on. You'll be okay, right?"

I nod.

The line moves quickly. Soon a young woman in a fur-trimmed red dress leads me to the throne, her hand gently resting on my back. Mama smiles as I sit on Santa's lap. He is large and his clothes rustle as he shifts to hold me. A cascade of white curls brushes against my face.

"Have you been good?" Santa asks.

Have I been good? I don't know what to say.

I look over at Mama. She watches with a smile.

"Of course you have!" he laughs. "Have you decided what you want for Christmas?" he whispers to me.

I lean in and whisper into the curls that I really want a Lionel train like the boys in my family have, and that I'll really take good care of it, and another doll would be okay, too. He laughs and gives me a hug before he sends me back to Mama.

I return, and Mama quickly leans down to me. "Did you tell him what you wanted?"

"Yes."

"What did you tell him?"

"I can't tell you, Mama. I told him."

Mama smiles, sighs, and shakes her head.

On hot and humid summer days, Mama and I set out for the park across the gorge. Nay Aug Park has a zoo, a swan pond, a mine, a penny arcade, a pool that has a sand bottom, and a museum. Everything in the park but the penny arcade is free, and the Everhart Museum is open all year round, so Mama and I go there a lot. Mama takes me to the pool even though she doesn't swim. Instead, she takes a break in the dark green Adirondack chairs lined up under the shade trees all along it.

To get to the park we walk the back alleys of our neighborhood to reach the crossing stoplight where Highway 307 swings steeply down into our valley from the east. While we wait for the light to change, I look at the brick houses across the highway and shudder. The row of identical houses is a set with pieces missing. The empty lots between the houses show where runaway trucks have lost control coming down the mountain highway—always at this place. Mama and I talk about it a lot.

"Yeah, honey," Mama says. We walk across the road, hand in hand. "It's too bad about those houses." She shrugs. "It's a steep road and the brakes on those trucks don't always work."

Ahead is the Harrison Avenue Bridge and the always-thrilling crossing over the gorge. Mama, I know, is already thinking of the mainline tracks that run beneath the bridge.

"Maybe we'll see a train," Mama says cheerfully.

As Mama and I walk onto the bridge, I look through the urn-shaped cement balusters to see the ravine and waterfalls of the Roaring Brook below. We walk impossibly high above the treetops that grow on the upstream side. I hold on tight to Mama's hand. Almost at the other side of the bridge, we are suspended above the mainline Delaware, Lackawanna, & Western Railroad tracks.

Downstream in the distance we can see the gray, stone passenger station at the edge of downtown, and we hear the thrumming begin as the locomotives ready to leave. The sound changes as they pull out. Waves of thrumming grind slowly at first, then tighter and tighter, as if the sound is tightened like the spring of a mechanical toy being wound turn by turn. Yellow-nosed locomotives are coming our way. Mama checks car traffic on the bridge and pulls on my arm.

"Let's go see!" she says. I know what's coming—I am

frightened—and yet I can't resist. We step down off the upstream sidewalk, clatter over two lanes of asphalt, and up onto the downstream sidewalk over the rails and wait. The staccato thrumming bounces against the walls of the ravine, over the water and across to the tracks on the other side. An extra hum rides atop the engine's sound like a siren.

"It's coming!" I shout. "It's a coal train!"

It reaches the bridge, and we become part of the train. Between the balusters, I bend and wave. The engineer waves back as the lead yellow engine passes beneath us. The sound crashes into the bridge. Mama quickly turns and checks that there's no car traffic behind us. "Let's run!" she shouts, pointing back to the upstream side. She grabs me to make a wild dash back across the bridge, chasing those locomotives upgrade. We clatter down onto the road, jump up to the far sidewalk, and land against the upstream balusters. Looking down between them we watch the locomotives emerge, black, oily smoke veiling their tops. For a fraction of a second, we are on top of the locomotives and can pretend we are riding them upgrade, heading for the tunnels around the bend. We travel along for only a few seconds, but the feeling is so strong, we are nothing but train.

The connection breaks. We let go of the thrumming beasts, and they go around the bend. We watch the string of black coal cars emerge one by one beneath us, their anthracite black diamonds shiny in the sunlight, like dark sugar crystals. Cars *rattle rattle rattle* upgrade, sounding like coal, roaring coal, the coal rattling down the chute into our coalben. Coal going away. Our coal. Going to some other city. Some power plant. Some factory. Some truck. Somebody's basement. We watch speechless. A wheel here and there in a long line of metal and carbon steel sounds like a bell struck and held. The lead locomotives have pushed on past the bend and through the tunnel; their sound becomes mute and still the cars come. Black coal car beads on an immense thread follow along around the bend and through the tunnel until they, too, vanish. The rattling becomes a wind that goes on and on until the thrumming comes from the pushers, the locomotives that power the train from behind the caboose until the train reaches the mountain ridge. They pass, grinding upgrade and around the bend, ending our connection. All that's left is a trailing roar, then silence.

All at once, I wish I could go with them.

"Can we ride on a train?"

"No, no. We can't," says Mama, shaking her head.

"But Mama, *you* got to ride…"

"That's because my people worked for the railroad. That was a long time ago." She pauses. "I don't think there'll be any passenger trains anywhere much longer." Mama shrugs her shoulders. "People want cars." Still holding my hand, Mama looks to me. "Ready to go?"

I nod and we turn toward the end of the bridge and finish our crossing.

III. LIGHT AND SHADOW: BOY AND COAL

In Iness's Lackawanna Valley the little engine huffs its way up, up, out of the valley so green. Lazily leaning on his elbow, the boy in the straw hat sits watching the little train make its way upgrade. Downhill from the boy, tree stumps fill a pasture bounded by wooden fences, separating the boy and a dirt road from the iron rails. In the far pasture beyond the rails, a few cows graze and rest.

Frozen in time, in pigment and turpentine, a moment is caught and held in suspension—I imagine it as the moment before the sound of the chuffing locomotive overrides the voices of the river, the tree leaves stirring in a breeze, the cows lowing in the pasture. The locomotive has already cut across the river and will break away from the flow pattern of the valley's waters, the traditional pattern of human transportation. It passes through clumps of trees, ignoring water altogether.

This is the crossroads. The dream of industry unfolds. The scene changes. Machines begin to chug, grind, and turn with speed and force beyond the power of wood and water. Brick by brick, a city will rise, pavers create avenues of the downtown while factories and warehouses will spring up along bands of rails, ever more rails. The newly-arrived, mostly immigrants from Eastern Europe, will submit and become submerged into veins of coal. They'll break the veins, shatter the coal, and send it upward. Their sons will sort it, sitting along sloping metal chutes in breaker buildings. Cold, barely able to breathe, unable to do anything but sit and sort, they will spend their childhoods. Many of the breaker boys will be maimed. Some of them will lose their lives by getting caught in the machinery. And others will leave the breakers, be promoted to working with mules in the mines, or will be chosen to become spraggers, to sit in coal-lined darkness, opening and closing doors for mine carts. All this great machinery of metal and flesh will be set in motion so that trains will be powered, bringing coal away, up out of the valley to fuel forges, factories, and other trains; to carry more people, paving more of the land to receive more immigrants.

By the end of the nineteenth century, the Lackawanna Valley will be an industrial center. The population of the valley will grow. Investors and owners will attain fantastic wealth, will build ornate architectural edifices for their homes and businesses while miners and their families will live in company houses—no more than shacks with no running water. Mine owners will dwell in mansions away from the river and mines while their workers will live beside rails and culm dumps. Five rail lines will converge in the deep Lackawanna Valley, offering destinations in all directions while serving their main purpose: to extract as much coal from the valley as possible, paying the lowest wages and tariffs, sometimes building rails aloft through the city on trestles, over streets and houses at the oddest locations and angles imaginable.

The city will become taller, gothic, ornate. Steel-reinforced structures will stretch skyward, glass will reflect gray light and smoky skies, and blue sparks of electricity will flash on trolley wires. All these dreams will unfold on the Lackawanna Valley floor while the valley's veins are drained of anthracite and their stores of ancient sunlight are brought to the surface. Blackness blossoms along every byway and in lungs and hearts throughout each and every dwelling along the banks of the Lackawanna River.

In pigment and oils, George Inness captured the crossroads between dirt road and steel rails, between wood- and coal-driven economies, between horse- or water-powered transportation and the age of coal and steel, between agrarian and urban landscapes.

Yet nowhere in Inness's *The Lackawanna Valley* can be seen the veins of black coal that make possible the iron smelting used to build a city and produce rails for an entire nation. You do not see anthracite and its waste, culm, piled on the landscape, four stories high. And nothing in the painting depicts the mines or miners underground.

Looking carefully, though, you can find the black coal in the center of the painting, in the many cars pulled along by the locomotive. Though the locomotive burns wood and crosses a wooden bridge, coal will power the forges of Lackawanna Iron to build more rails and locomotives and provide iron for bridges. Coal is about to leave the valley and bring mass production and the machinery of industry to life.

I look at the painting, and I want to shout, *Stop! Stop now before it's too late! Don't bring that coal up to the surface...*

—

As a girl I would stare at a copy of *The Lackawanna Valley* in a book at school, believing the story it told, wanting the perfection of the scene—everything in its place, all needs met. I longed to be in a landscape as beautiful as I perceived the Lackawanna Valley in the painting to be—wished for my own landscape to look like that once more—if indeed it ever did. All I saw up and down the valley were burning conical mountains of coal waste, smoking and rusty pink by day and covered in blue flames at night. Smoke filled the valley, and we breathed sulfurous air odored like rotten eggs. Our wooden clapboard houses were dirty. Our alleys and roadways were black with cinders. Our slate sidewalks tilted crazily. And there was the ever-present sound of locomotives grinding against steep grade, up and out.

I look at a copy of the painting. I wonder about the boy in the scene, forever watching, perhaps chewing on a straw as the locomotive wends its way towards him across the river. Would he dare touch the rails to feel the vibration, awed by the power of the machine? Does he feel spied upon by the locomotive that crosses the river and pasture?

What if we could see his face?

Perhaps the boy dreams of faraway places, wondering if he might ride a train out and away. Or perhaps he is more down-to-earth, thinking the train a silly machine and folks should leave transport to horses.

Perhaps if the boy were born half a century later, his pasture gone, he might work in a breaker, or in a mine.

—

When I was a girl, the boy's world in the Inness painting filled me with longing. I lingered in the scene. Even as the iron rails were expanding out onto the landscape, and the Inness painting celebrated the movement of iron and coal, the boy's territory was composed of living things and materials gathered from woods and fields: split-rail fences, the boy's hat woven from straw, his linen shirt from flax. I wanted to sit next to the boy gazing on tree stumps and grazing cattle, and I wanted something from that scene— the greenness and meadow, the open space, the beautifully leafed-out trees—the palette of early summer. I didn't have the words for it then: the *pastoral landscape*, the *bucolic*. I wanted *that*. Not the landscape of the Lackawanna Valley in my time, covered by rails, roads of asphalt, clapboard houses sinking into the mines, fires raging beneath our city, burning culm dumps, and acrid smoke. Perhaps I imagined that I could, like Lewis Carroll's Alice, step into Inness's scene, into all its glorious pastel colors, so appealing, so clean.

I wanted something sweet that likely never existed.

And even as I felt the magic and sweetness in the Inness painting, I felt an uneasiness, too. There was a shadowy memory in my childhood of a second image, a black-and-white photograph of the same scene that I remembered seeing in a book, and I felt unsettled by it. *What about the other picture?* I asked my teachers and librarians.

No one seemed to remember it.

Diamonds

"Diamonds," I whisper.

Whirling white snowflakes fall faster and thicker, glittering as they catch the light of the streetlamp. From the dark perch of my parents' bedroom window I watch the snowfall while the radiator in the corner hisses. I can see the whole street most of the way down to the bottom of the hollow. Beyond that, there is only snow. There is neither creek at the bottom of our hill nor mountain rising above it. No houses exist beyond the ones across the street. The world ends at the top of our hill—there is no great valley carpeted with houses dropping for a mile beyond it. Black culm, collieries, and rails vanish. The rumbles and bangs from the valley disappear. Snow hides the hummocks in our yard, and everywhere it buries the blackness of coal. Snow blankets and muffles all but the thrumming of departing coal trains tonight, and even the throb of the pushing and pulling engines is somehow dulled.

I open the window just a little, to touch the snow—to hear it shushing.

"*Phohhhh*," says the wind.

"*Cheeeeeshshh*," answers the radiator in the corner.

I put my fingers through the open window, and I reach out to touch crystals. Diamonds, I pretend. They melt in my hand, leaving it full of droplets reflecting the light of the streetlamp.

Diamonds.

"If you have diamonds, you are rich!" I have heard my family say.

I think about the gold band on Grandma's hand. In the center of the ring, a raised gold heart holds a diamond. It glitters as her blue-veined hands push her red-handled rolling pin into dough.

One supper at our house, I ask Mama and Dad about it.

"Grandma wears a diamond. Is she rich?"

"No, honey," Dad answers. "It's only a chip of a diamond."

Mama laughs quietly. "Grandma is *not* rich!" She pauses. "And neither are we," she says shrugging her shoulders.

"Why do married people have diamonds?"

"Well, I guess they're durable. Pure."

"Are there *black* ones?"

"Well…" Mama hesitates, "There're *black* diamonds… but that's *coal*."

Dad answers now. "A diamond is a gemstone. But *black* diamonds—that's another name for anthracite."

"Anthracite?"

"Yeah. Black diamonds. It's hard coal. Burns hot and clean."

"*Clean?*"

"Well…less smoky. There are ashes. But it's good coal for heating. That's why we use it to heat our house and Grandma's house. And anthracite is used to make our electricity. It's burned in big furnaces."

"Like ours?"

"No. No, really big. And really hot. The anthracite burns hotter than other kinds of coal because it's hard coal."

◆ ◆ ◆

And black.

So black that when I grow up and move away from the valley, my sense of color is skewed.

Before we travel to the Lackawanna Valley to pick up pieces of furniture and bring them to our home in the Midwest, I tell my husband about an end table that an uncle made—probably from pear wood—very blonde, and my mama's sewing machine, which I remember as a light mahogany color.

On the journey in the Lackawanna Valley, I am amazed to find blackness is everywhere, lining all the roads still, even though the culm dumps and the breaker buildings have been leveled. My place of origin is a palette of dark hues. I return to my new home in the Midwest stunned to discover that the end table my uncle made is really a deep brown color, and my mama's sewing machine is the color of black walnuts. Amid the blackness of the Lackawanna Valley landscape, the browns of the wooden furniture seemed pale.

—

In school in the Lackawanna Valley, we learned many things by rote. Because of who we were and when we were, we learned the evolution of coal:

> lignite, bituminous, anthracite
>
> lignite　　bituminous　anthracite
>
> lignite…coal that's practically peat moss
>
> bituminous…soft coal
>
> anthracite…hard coal

We learned which is best (anthracite, of course, used for heating homes), and that nearly all the anthracite in the United States is found in Eastern Pennsylvania where we live. But no teachers could explain why the Glenn Alden Colliery in Scranton would want to sell coal covered in blue dye as blue coal.

Somewhere in my memory, though, a voice rings out at some gathering—perhaps Dad's voice, because he read all the time from science and science fiction, magazine after magazine, as he waited for the alarm to sound at the fire station. Or perhaps it's the voice of one of his brothers, who hauled coal in a big truck.

"You know, coal is carbon—but diamonds are carbon, too."

"Get outta here."

"Yeah. Coal is carbon and diamonds are pure carbon."

Probably there's a snort in response. And my response was to turn it over and over inside me: Is it possible—such a transformation (though I didn't know that word yet)—from coal to diamonds?

The voices swirl around me.

"Yep, gemstones someday. Not yet. Black diamonds. That's all we have: *black* diamonds. It's the only riches we got."

Someone erupts into laughter.

"And all we do is haul it up, send it away, and burn it."

Burning it.

Anthracite heated our houses and made the radiators hiss. It burned in huge furnaces to make steel, and burned to make our electricity.

Dad's voice rises out of my memory:

"That's what makes us The Electric City," he says, and I'm lying on the wide, soft backseat of my family's latest used car, looking up through the windows at a tall downtown building topped by a huge flashing sign. The round metal frame that holds all the lightbulbs is flanked by electric light torches. Lights in the center of the wreath come on a few at a time to spell words: *The Electric City*. It's like having Christmas all year.

"Why do they have those words?" I ask.

"The Electric City? Because they want to advertise that Scranton was a special place a long time ago. It's because of black diamonds."

Mama's and Dad's voices float over me.

"We used to have electric streetcars."

"The first ones in the country."

"But they're gone now," says Mama.

"Black diamonds?"

"No, honey, streetcars. All we have is buses now. So noisy. Smelly." Mama sighs and shakes her head. "What a shame. There's so much gone now."

◆ ◆ ◆

The streetlamp light catches on one corner of the silver radiator in the dark bedroom. The radiator hisses and chugs from black diamonds burning in our basement, sending steam banging up through the pipes. Beyond the white window frame, snow covers our street with white diamonds only until the cindering trucks arrive the next morning, as they always do, and stain the snow yellow with coal ash.

For a moment at the window ledge, I push my index finger into the cold, wet snow, tracing the shapes of diamonds. I want to fly out the window and dance a snow dance, spinning and whirling, catching, and gathering the glittering crystals so we can be rich.

Coal Year

Here I come a rumbling, rumbling,
Please may I come in?
Now my coal is tumbling, tumbling,
Tumbling in the bin.

—The Coal Man

Fall

"Coal Man's coming today," says Mama as she pulls the broom in swift, short strokes across the kitchen floor. I prance on bare tiptoes over the marbled turquoise linoleum tiles, its tidal pools swirling at my feet. I sway as I cross to the rag-rug islands in front of the stove, sink, and back door.

It's September, and it's still green down our hollow, but Mama's anxious to have the coalben filled. Who knows when a cold spell might come? Already in the gathering dark of evenings, the clouds sail in, dense purple-gray, meaning cold is coming. This morning, though, is sunny and warm. That's hard on Mama. She longs to take a walk, but stays home, waiting for the Coal Man.

Midmorning, I hear the coal truck—a large, loud monster. It pounds down our steep street and comes to a slow metal-screeching halt in front of our house. All the coal trucks have screeching brakes—no matter whose you hire. This one is blue, coated in a film of oily black so thick that the name on the door is unreadable. From my front porch rail perch all I can do is watch. Mama has told me to stay away from strangers.

The Coal Man jumps down from his truck and comes around the back of his rig.

"You call for coal?" he shouts and flashes a gap-tooth grin. He drops a cigarette on the street and crushes it with his heel.

I nod, then turn and run for Mama. "Coal Man's here!" I shout, banging the front screen door. "Mama!"

She takes off her apron and descends to the basement to open the coalben door, then climbs into the nearly empty coalben beneath the porch at the front of the house. She pushes the three-paned glass window outward, propping it open with a stick.

I return to the porch cautiously now, feeling exposed. I stay behind the rail and wrap my arms around the white-painted pillar to watch. The Coal Man pulls his truck out perpendicularly in the street and jockeys the truck into position. Backing the truck over boulevard grass and side-walk, the Coal Man bumps his truck against the cinder-cement wall. The tilt is stunning. He leaps from the cab, and lets the door slam shut, pulled by the downward slant of the hill. From the rack at the truck's bumper, the Coal Man pulls out boards and rocks to prop the wheels at the front and back of the truck to keep it in place. Back to the cab he goes, raises the truck bed, and races to the back end for the ramps. He slides oily black steel ramps across the yard, hooking one end to the back of the truck. The other end pushes into the coalben under the front porch. It's tricky getting the truck in just the right place so that once the ramps are out, they go straight to the little window. On Grandma's street, the coal truck has less of a tilt, but her coal man has to ramp over her hedge. Oh, her coal man grumbles if her hedge hasn't been trimmed low enough.

Coal Man wastes no time. Up goes the little chute door at the top of the ramps and out comes the coal: a rattling, rushing torrent of black diamonds. The downpour is deafening, and all I can see is a blur of black.

Coal Man checks the flow of coal at the ramp's top. Confident of the constant stream, he leaves the truck and goes around to the back of our house, to the basement door. I follow. His long strides take him quickly across the basement floor to the coalben where he watches the coal come in. Grabbing a shovel and hopping over the half-planked wall, he flings coal left and right to fill the corners of the room. As the bin fills, the space between the coal and the ceiling shrinks, and Coal Man's head hits the porch joists. Out he comes, and he and Mama put in the next planks. The coal continues filling. Mama adds more planks until the plank wall is now as high as Mama's collarbone—as high as it will be all year. Later, Mama will reach in and shovel the coal surface level so that it will be easier to work with. Coal Man wipes his face on his filthy sleeve and heads back outdoors.

As Mama hurries upstairs to find the money envelope, I follow her.

"Mama, where did he get the coal from?"

"What do you mean, *where*?"

"Where did he get it from for the truck?"

"From the breaker. You know. From the breaker—down in the Flats," she says, and hurries to her bedroom closet. She reaches into the small, dark space and retrieves the worn electric company envelope marked **COAL**. From it she takes and counts the sixty-three dollars it has taken all year to save up for this expense. She sighs, puts back the envelope, and carries the cash away downstairs.

I don't like breaker buildings. Breakers are towers of blackness, surrounded by blackness—the mountains of culm dumps towering over them. Each breaker is a lopsided black building shaped like a stack of alphabet blocks, with one little last block off-center on top, many-windowed—or it would be many-windowed except most of the panes are broken. And the whole place clatters so loud. Dad took me down to the breakers in the Flats along the Lackawanna River, and we had to shout to one another—you can't get close to one and still talk. Though I couldn't see inside the building, I was frightened of it. The breaker building stood dark and tall, and there was something about it I knew was really bad—but I couldn't name what it is. Dad told me there used to be breaker boys who sat inside breakers in the cold and dark along metal chutes, breathing coal dust and sorting coal. Sometimes they came away maimed. But that was a long time ago—when my dad's dad was a boy. Now there are only machines inside. I still don't understand how it all works.

"Mama, how do they get the coal into the truck?"

Mama waves her hand in the air as if brushing away a fly. "I don't know, honey. I've never seen how. Ask your dad." She dashes out the door.

With an oily black broom, Coal Man sweeps the last of the black diamonds from the truck bed through the chute. Sparse beads of coal rattle down the ramp and sound the end of the downpour. Coal Man pulls up the ramps, stacks them back on the truck, and hangs up his broom. He wipes his hands on a rag before pulling out a receipt book from the cab. Mama brings up the cash and hands it over. The truck heads out into the street and grinds uphill. Mama pulls the prop from the coalben window. The coal year has begun.

Winter

"I got to shovel coal," Mama says each winter evening after pouring the thickest portion of hot coffee from the bottom of the chrome percolator. She sets her white porcelain mug at the end of the table and crosses to the cellar door. At the cellarway landing she pauses and takes the coarse navy cardigan from its nail. It is one of Dad's fireman sweaters shrunk too small for him to wear. Mama is happy to have it to protect her from the chill of the cellar in wintertime. She flicks on the light for the bottom landing. "It's so damp," she says to herself as she descends the wooden stairs. Even though the bulb is lit, the cellar is shadowy dark. I follow close to Mama, daring the night demons to get me while she is with me.

Across from us, the square, steel furnace lies in wait, a rumbling beast. All day, all night, the grinding sound of the furnace beast in the cellar seeps through our floors. A humming, throbbing, crackle-crunching sound as if the beast has teeth. Ours is a newer model furnace. Its mottled blue-steel coat is smooth and shiny, its corners rounded with silvery chrome. Beside it sits its source of sustenance: anthracite coal in a black metal drum, the hopper, attached by a black iron umbilicus. I pause beside it and listen. There it is—a crunching sound. Something is eating the coal in there…some kind of animal…

"Mama, why does it make that sound?"

"What sound do you mean? The burning?"

"The sound in the tube…"

"Oh. It's the *worm*." (This is what she always says. It makes no sense.)

"A worm? You mean *worms*?" I see in my mind's eye worms, moist and wiggly…

"No, not like the worms we dig up for fishing at the mountain lake. It's a giant screw, like. It pulls the coal into the fire."

A giant screw turning day and night, pulling coal to the roaring belly of the beast. I stare at the tube trying to imagine its insides. This furnace is *alive*—I can feel it, though no one else seems to notice.

On one end of the furnace is the peephole above the ash can door. I can slide the cover sideways to see if the coal is burning. It always is. Always. But not always with orange flames—sometimes with blue flames like the ones on the kitchen gas stove, or on the culm dumps. Peeping into the furnace frightens me. The beast might catch me spying and devour me, too…instead, there's a shout.

"Get away from there! It's *hot*. What are you *doing*?" Mama stares at me. I quickly slide the cover back in place.

"Dad checks it sometimes…"

"Leave it alone."

Sometimes the beast is a warm bosom for baby animals. When we find abandoned tiny bunnies outside in spring, or fledgling birds injured by our tomcat, Dad tenderly packs them in a low, cardboard box. He tries to feed them. After tucking rags around them, he places the box on top of the furnace to keep them warm through the night. "We'll see if they make it," he tells me. Each time I pray hard at my bedside for their protection, and pray to find them well in the morning. "Dear Jesus…" I cross myself, pleading on their behalf. But each time when morning light comes, we descend into the basement to find our babies stiff and cold, and I weep of a broken heart. The beast is no mother. It offers no fur or downy feathers or quick heartbeat. Its smooth steel skin coats a belly that makes ash and belches sulfur smoke.

Our blue beast is not nearly as frightening as Grandma's. In her tiny house, the narrow, wooden plank steps lead down from the door in the kitchen to two low-ceilinged, dirt-floored rooms. Right there, close to the bottom of the steps, lies Grandma's beast.

A *she*-beast, so clearly: a narrow waist defining her broad, circular bosom and hips. *She*, plastered with a coat of flaky asbestos, yellowed and stained with age like old women's teeth. So raggedy. A snow of ivory asbestos lies all around her on the black dirt. *She*, with a black iron grill for her belly and inside, behind the isinglass window, her flames flicker wildly, consuming coal, casting orange, pointy lights on the gray, whitewashed walls. No worm for her umbilicus. No umbilicus. Dad and his brothers alternate the job of feeding her each day, hand-shoveling the coal into her belly. Ravenous, she takes it all, reducing it before another morning into large flaky ash clumps. Nothing we kids can imagine in our black-and-orange Halloween nightmares can match the horrific image of Grandma's basement beast, consuming.

I asked Mama about why the coal in Grandma's coalben is so much bigger than ours. She told me it was because it was Chestnut-size coal and that we use Pea coal at our house, and that different sizes of coal have different names—Pea, Chestnut, or Buckwheat. To me, they don't look like any of those things.

Mama crosses the basement floor to the coalben, and near its door quickly slips into worn fireman boots, shoes and all, not bothering to close the ladder-shaped buckles. Setting the hodpail aside, she swings open the coalben door. Mama reaches in with a shovel, pulling the rattling Pea coal forward toward the planking. Coal rolls down from the sides and piles up against the door. Urged by the shovel, coal rattles and rolls like beads unstrung. Mama stabs with the shovel and flings the coal out, spraying it into the hod with a BANG! She rocks forward in the floppy boots. She stabs, flings, and BANG! Two shovels-full fill the hod. Mama leans the shovel against the plank wall and crosses the floor to the hopper, dumps the hodpail, and heads back for more. Mama races with the hod, and I stretch up on tiptoe and peek into the hopper. Ever-so-slowly the coal swirls and slides downward into the worm, and then into the belly of the furnace. A coal landscape is left behind in the hopper: an upside-down conical mountain of air—a negative sculpture of the conical culm dumps that cover our landscape everywhere. BANG! Mama continues her race. Nine times she crosses. Nine hods to the hopperful and now she tops it off for the night. Done. The hopper is full level.

"Come on," she says.

Greasy blackness covers Mama's hands and sweater. She slips out of the rubber boots, crosses back to the steps. I follow closely at her heels and slip ahead of her on the stairs to leave the dark basement behind. At the top landing, she takes off the navy sweater and puts it back on the nail. Satisfied to have her chore done, Mama sighs and reenters the kitchen and the world of light. She reaches for a washcloth to remove the coal dust from her face and hands, then reaches for her mug on the table. She takes a good slurp of her now-warm coffee. I look in the chrome mirror of the percolator. In the percolator shines all the world behind us—a cellar door, the pantry and backdoor, the rag rugs ashore along the bottoms of the doors, keeping the cold drafts out.

Spring

Ring around a-rosy,
pocket full of posies
Ashes, ashes, we all fall down.

Ashes fill our land everywhere—from the mountainous piles of burning culm, to the cinders lining our alleys, to the coal ash spewed from our furnaces.

Ashes, ashes...

"Why do we fall down, Mama?"

Mama pauses and scrunches up her face. "It's death, like," she says to me. "Ashes of death, you know. Like Lent ashes, where the priest says, remember? 'Ashes to ashes, dust to dust.'"

Inside the furnace, coal turns to ash: white, rust, and gray. It falls into the square metal can below the grate. Mama pulls the can out every two days or so, scraping the cement floor with the heavy load. Ash dust always comes out in a cloud and fills the basement air. It seeps upward through the floorboards to live with us; dust around the edges of the living room carpet that only covers the unvarnished middle of the wooden floor. Mama cleans the yellowy varnished floor around it crawling on her hands and knees. Every day she orbits the threadbare wool carpet, so worn that its red-blue-yellow paisley design is mostly a crisscross of amber straw. Every day she wipes away the fine powdery ash. But she cannot wipe it all away. Fine ash from the bones of coal fills the air we breathe.

Dust within us, dust all around us. We even use coal ashes in our food.

In summertime, Grandpa, Mama's Tha, takes the coal ashes he's saved to his enormous garden. He sifts coal

ashes through his fingers as tarry ashes fall from his cigar.
Dad and I stand with him.

"You put ashes like this, eh?" He grunts the question to
me and Dad. We squat with Grandpa looking at mounds of
powdery gray dust beneath each plant. A fine coat of ash
covers the dark green leaves at each thick-stemmed plant.
I don't know what my dad really thinks, but he listens by
looking downward, showing respect to his father-in-law,
the patriarch. "You put ashes...no bugs," says Grandpa. He
nods to agree with himself. At home, Dad sprinkles more
fine coal ash on the tomato plants Tha had given him. Even
touching the hairy tomato plants, I can smell and taste the
lemony, sulfurous ashes.

Trash day, ash day. Our blue furnace beast gives us ashes
to tote. On a sleety day in early spring, Mama puts on her
wool coat and rubber boots. I do the same. "Come on," she
says. "It might turn to ice." She means the weather. Her
fears of falling outdoors while toting ash cans hasten her
steps. Her twisted left arm reminds her to be cautious. And
if she broke it again, the doctor told her at the state hospital, she could lose it. We descend to the cellar and cross
the cement floor to the furnace. Below the peephole on the
furnace beast is its ash door: wide, heavy, and latched with
a chrome handle. Mama bends down and swings it open.
"Watch out!" she says, pushing me back. With a grunt, she
pulls on the rectangular loop of steel wire and coaxes the
can out the opening. She drags it onto the hollow carved
into the cement floor from the scraping of many heavy
cans, and it lands with a bump on the uneven floor, a fine
cloud of white ash rising to meet us. I look in the furnace

for live coals burning orange amid the black cinders. They fill me with delight, these dark jewels.

Just two of us, mother and daughter, lift the can in unison with a grunt. My side of the can is much closer to the ground than Mama's. She doesn't mind. Without my help, she'd have to drag the cans through the basement and the length of the house to the street. She has me, though, and so we struggle together. The huge heavy can puts little more space between us than a bushel basket. We swing, we grunt, we scrape and bruise our legs against the can's metal edges as we wobble across the basement floor. We squeeze through the door one at a time and lift the can up the step to the walk at the side of our house. It is an awfully long way to the street at the front of the house. By now it's pelting sleet that melts as soon as it hits the cinder-cement surface. All along our house's cellar wall, the lily leaves lie wilted and ice coated. High above them, long icicle daggers hang precariously from the eaves. We are wary, but we cannot look up from our burden. We must concentrate. We must look ahead, trying to keep our rhythm lest we scrape the heavy can against our legs.

We reach the front wall. We go up three large cement steps to the landing, and leave the safety of its flat surface to cross the steeply sloping sidewalk and grassy boulevard. We begin the crossing, walking gingerly in case of unseen ice. I'm on the downhill side this time and it's dreadful. I drop my end. The can tips, mimicking the slope of our hill, and the ashes slide downhill within the can. Mama straightens up suddenly with an angry scowl on her face until she realizes that we've gotten our usual positions mixed up. She moves around to the other side of the can.

"Come on," she says, more gently, and we try to lift again. "Huh," we say as we pull upward. Just a few more steps and we plunk the can down next to the street. We back away from the rising dust puffs out of habit, but the steady sleet has already quenched it. Returning quickly, we head back to the basement for the remaining cans and the one wet, paper grocery bag of trash.

An hour or so later, big men come with the ash truck. I watch from Mama's bedroom window as the men slow the truck in front of our house. The man in back takes a can with his two big hands and with one strong swift motion lifts it up, flips it to dump the contents, and bangs the can down. He empties the others quickly, rough, and so strong.

At morning's end, Mama picks up the now dented cans and carries them back the length of the building to the basement beast.

Summer

August is hot, humid, and rainy. Mama heads for the basement to ready the ben for the coal year's end. We have to push the coal from the corners to the door where we can get at it easier. Dressed in work overalls and firemen boots and armed with a shovel, Mama gets ready to climb in. She buckles the latches on the boots this time. Behind her in the only jeans I own, orange pedal pushers, and a huge man's flannel shirt, I reach for my small, red snow shovel. "No," says Mama, "Here. Take this one. Your shovel's too small." She hands me a long, rounded scooping shovel, the one with the missing corner. It's taller than I am by half.

"It's got a tight handle," Mama says. She steps over the low planking, into the ben, and reaches out a hand for me. Holding onto her, I swing my legs as best I can over the plank wall and drag my shovel with me.

Mama and I stand side by side on the bumpy surface of coal. At this time of year, it's hard to get enough coal in one stab to fill the hodpail. With the coal ben almost empty, we begin to see the cement floor. Mama and I pull the coal toward the door. The shovel's edges bounce against the coal, which clatters and cascades like beads. Our arms are shaken with each pull. It's so loud. Slippery, too, as we try to work around the coalben. And with each movement, the air fills with coal dust. We pull and pile coal. We pant. We scrape the bottom and rattle our shovels until our teeth chatter and our heads ring.

Done. The silence is stunning. The light through the small glass windows shows the rising powder of black coal dust. Outdoors, in the world of light and summer heat, cicadas buzz. We stand in the silence of the coal-dark ben, covered in sooty black, huffing. We breathe the blackness into our bodies and sigh, satisfied with our work.

Buried

"What should we do?" my best friend, Nita, asks.

Mama is hanging laundry in the wet spring air. Nita is in the house with me. Mama thinks she can leave us alone together. At the age of eight, Nita is two years older than me.

"We could go in the attic and play house," Nita suggests.

We climb the stairs to the second floor, and then up the attic stairs. The attic has been our playhouse all fall through winter, but now, in spring, as we reach the top of the stairs, the heat held under the roof takes our breath away. It feels as if we've walked into the furnace room at school.

"Oh!" says Nita. "This won't work. It's too hot."

"The basement is cooler."

We head down to the basement. Nita looks over to the coalben door.

"Let's…go into the coalben!"

"Yeah. Let's!"

Deep down, we know it's a place we're not supposed to be, and that makes the choice more exciting.

We slip on the oversized, floppy firemen boots, unhook the coalben door, and climb in over the planks. The coal in the bin is less than half full—just the right amount of coal for us to stand on without bumping our heads on the bottom of the porch floor. Coal tumbles downhill beneath the floppy boots as we climb the slope toward the window. We giggle and run faster, the coal slides down even faster.

We jump on top and slide down like we imagine kids on hay piles in a farmyard, though the sharp-edged coal bruises our bottoms and legs through our pants. We roll and sift coal through our hands, bury our legs as if we are in beach sand. Laughing, we toss coal upward. It comes down with the sound of hard rains. Our hands, our clothes, our faces get a shiny black sheen. Exhausted from laughing we fall back onto the slope of coal until we hear a voice.

"Where are you?" Mama calls. We can hear her muffled

voice outside the stone wall. We are stunned into silence. We hear footsteps on the porch above us. Then we hear the footsteps through the house. Nita and I stare wide-eyed at each other. Nita pushes her glasses back up on her nose.

"WHERE ARE YOU?" Mama's shout comes from the top cellar landing. We cannot get our buried feet out from the coal quickly enough to grab the door and shut it, even if there was a handle on our side. We hear Mama stop on the long steep descent to the basement. "You're NOT in the COALBEN!" We hear the panic edging her voice.

Sheepishly, we come to the door, and she gives us what for.

"What are you *doing*?" Even through her shock and horror, Mama goes quickly through her list. "Look at your hair! Your pants! You got coal in the boots! And you got coal pushed to the far end where I can't reach it! It has to be shoveled back. All my work! And now I have to do it over. And..." Mama pauses, her eyes wide, "you could have been *buried alive!*"

Nita climbs out slowly and doesn't look back at me. Mama sends Nita home, too angry and scared to say another word to her.

It's a tearful trip to the clawfoot tub upstairs for me—an extra bath for the week. After a harsh scrubbing and some harsh words, Mama sends me to bed until supper.

In my bedroom, the hot tears fall. It isn't any worse, I justify to myself, than what my uncles did! When they were kids they climbed into the mile-long train tunnel down the street. No one was supposed to go there. A train could come, and it did! And lucky for them, they found a hollow in the wall to pile into when the electric locomotive came. *That* was bad. Or the times they threw wooden factory crates with iron straps onto the electrified third rail to watch them blow up. They blew out all the signals down the line. *That* was bad. At least we didn't stop any trains.

Nita and I never go into the coalben together again, but a few years older and farther afield we continue climbing and sliding. Up and away from our houses and yards in the hollow, up the mountain, nearly to the top, we find our way into the woods to an old slag pile, three stories high. It is our very own secret pile, next to a hollowed-out building with rusty machinery next to a pond. Though it is an abandoned mine building, my imagination sees it as an old-fashioned mill with a millpond, just a bit run down. I feel happy and safe being there.

On the slag pile, we slip and stagger to our heart's content. There are, among the millions of fragments of broken rust, gray, and black rocks, some fossils. Nita and I become hunters, combing for treasure. A fossil print in stone. Perhaps pawprints, or insect imprints, or even plant images. We are unsure what we might find—until I discover something. It's a sharp-edged piece of slate: gray on one side, and rust-colored on the other. And on the russet face of the rock shard, there is a shallow black imprint of a plant. Mimosa-like ferny leaves. I hold the shard in my hand and look at it in wonder.

"What did you find?" Nita calls from farther upslope. She comes close, leans over, and pushes her glasses back against her nose. "How did you find it?" I gently stroke the image with my thumb and part of the image begins to rub off. The print, so durable, has lain hidden for millions of years, has been blasted from the layers underground, yet can be rubbed away by my fingers.

"How did you find it?" Nita asks again. I shrug. It's as if I've found something alive. I smile and put it in my pocket. "Where were you?" she asks. I point to the spot. Nita begins pawing through the shards.

I walk halfway up the slope and around to the right. I stop, look down, and see a very black, thin, smooth shard. Something about it calls to me. I turn it over to find another fern fossil—this one a very narrow leafy image. It gives off a faint shine against the smooth grain of the rock. I'm not sure if I can tell Nita this time.

"No fair," is what she says when she catches up to me. For the rest of the afternoon, Nita finds no fossils and grumbles. Without much effort, I notice certain shards, turn them over, and find more fossils, almost as if I can hear them. I don't tell Nita about this, for I can't explain my kinship with the dark prints.

School

"That's where you'll be," Mama points as we walk slate sidewalks along a series of Kelly green, tall iron bars. Between them, in flashes, I see a rough dark surface of asphalt stretching outward from a large, dark, gray brick building. All over the asphalt, children run and shout, all shouting different things at the same time. Jump ropes turn like beaters, slapping the ground. A brick-red utility ball hits the ground with the sound of a choked bell and a wheeze. *Wheee-UH*, says the ball.

Behind the children, wire mesh-covered basement windows rise out of the ground making the three-story building so tall that I must lean back to see the great slate shingles of its roof. At the very top, a curved metal tower rises like a thumb pointing to the sky, with rust-stained vents stacked along the stem of it.

I am uneasy. "In there? Why there, Mama?"

"You will be going to school in the fall. That's the school. So you can learn. Don't you want to learn?"

I want to learn to read books, but the building is like a big, gray castle. "I want to keep walking with you, Mama."

Mama doesn't answer. She walks along with a puzzled look on her face.

◆ ◆ ◆

All the children in our city of Scranton, Pennsylvania walked to neighborhood schools, castle-like stone-and-slate structures. They were edifices of the nineteenth-century belief in the power of education to bring the immigrants of my valley into the common language and values necessary to be Americans.

My memory takes me to the fall of 1964, when I was in first grade. The six-block walk on sunny days over dark, gray slate sidewalks was the sound of shoe leather slapping in a gathering of children from all the houses heading to school. We became a river with tributaries of all the neighborhood's children. I remember how beautiful the falling leaves of autumn were against the slate—many-colored red and yellow, splotched—how they felt waxy to the touch. We cradled color in our hands that blazed a contrast against the gray, ubiquitous houses and roads, the white-and-gray sky.

◆ ◆ ◆

The bell rings, and everyone on the rough asphalt is drawn into the lines at the school's front and side entrances. Just in time, I pass through the green gates and join everyone on broad flagstones leading to the stone archway. There's quiet except for shoe leather scuffling on sidewalks and a few furtive whispers. The lines become well-formed and silent. We pass through the massive wooden doors and up into the huge, darkened hallway.

In school at the beginning of the year, I learn to catch a

breath of air through the open windows while the dizzy-
ing smell of the newly applied, dark varnish dries on the
wainscoting, desks, and doors. I learn to use a cloakroom,
quickly taking off my wraps. I learn to hurry to my seat,
one in a series of ornate iron-and-wood desks perma-
nently bolted to the floor. I learn that we are surrounded
by slate in the form of sidewalks, roof tiles, and black-
boards. I learn to read and write and follow rules and bells
that bring us indoors and send us home twice a day. And
I learn that being good means following rules and bells.
Most importantly, I learn to move quickly and silently out
to the asphalt if the fire bell sounds.

In first grade, our reading books tell us stories about Alice
and Jerry. Jerry plays outdoors and runs with his dog, Jip.
Alice stays home, plays with dolls, and helps Mother. The
book tells us what we already know about who we are: girls
grow up to be housewives. If we are unlucky and can't find
a husband, we become old maids who'll work as nurses or
as teachers. To be a nurse or teacher when you grow up
means you have to go to college. Not a lot of girls do this.

Most of our daddies (if we still have them, alive) work
in a mine, a mill, or in the railyards. Our mamas stay home.
They don't drive anywhere. Cars are for daddies to go to
work or to drive us up the line or down the line to visit
relatives. The kids go to school and the kids go home for
lunch, walking to and from school four times each day.

Some mamas work in the garment mills while their
kids are in school. There are as many mills as schools, and
they are tall and made of bricks just like our schools except
that their roofs aren't as pretty and they don't have play-

grounds. Every school has a mill nearby, and when our school's windows are open we can hear the rattling of the sewing machines in the mill nearby.

In cold weather, radiators in the school knock and groan, filled with steam from a huge coal furnace in the basement—a furnace whose huge, white-bandaged pipes we see only when we descend to the lavatory. It looks like a giant spider kept in a cave. There are windows at the back of the classroom and tall windows on the side of the classroom, and they rattle with wind and become a drum from rain. Rain beats against the gray school, blurring the view of the white and gray sky. Even with all the ceiling lamps lit on a fall day, all light is drained into the dark wainscoting and floors. Especially in a fog. The street-lights come on.

On wet days, woolens drip onto the blackened, unvarnished floor of the divided cloakrooms, their scent wafting into the back of the classroom from the cloakroom doorway. The scent floats atop the background of varnish, coaldust (stronger smelling in wet weather), hot radiators, and graphite pencils. It mixes with the scents of rich chocolate milk, souring white milk, and the smell of a child who hasn't had a bath and wears mismatched clothes, joining our class for perhaps a few weeks, disappearing before the autumn leaves are off the trees.

This room in our school is like every other. All that changes from one year to the next is the direction of the sunlight and the teacher at the front of the classroom. Above the blackboard on one side, the faded, framed print of Abraham Lincoln balances that of George Washington. Mr. Lincoln looks off in the distance to where we can't see, while George Washington looks down his nose at us. Columns of desks put us in order for the teachers. Our knees bump against them. Whenever I can, I search on desks for the names of my relations, who sat in each of the same classrooms throughout two generations before me and carved their marks into the glossy wood. It's a secret pleasure to know that they were here before me and were so bold, though I would never do such a thing. I wonder what they thought about as they used the now-empty inkwells to fill their fountain pens and practice their penmanship.

After a song, the Pledge of Allegiance, and a silent prayer, the teacher takes attendance, calling out our names although we sit in alphabetical order. Because my name is at the end of the alphabet, I will always get to sit near the windows.

Sometimes we stand beside our desks and exercise to a phonograph record. But the best time of day is art time, either coloring a shape made with purple lines on a mimeo handout or cutting shapes from colored construction paper.

Our teacher takes construction paper and glue from the corner cupboard. She passes out the paper and serves us bottles of mucilage from metal trays. We giggle. *Mucilage.* From horses' hooves, we were told. Our minds' eyes see factories of boiling gray bone matter making slow amber, smelling sweet, slightly like old wooden beams in our mining valley houses, old houses that have seen the old horses our families talked about. We grip the heavy bottles by their waists, pointing their brick-red rubber nibs at each other. We push on the nibs and crack open the crusted glue at the worn slit. We lift and tilt the bottles, brushing away the gritty amber grains, smearing glue. Our fingers caress the nib, opening rubber lips. We place thumbs and forefingers on either side of the rubber tip, and we squeeze it and make its mouth open and close. We become ventriloquists. The nib sings like Frankie Valli's Four Seasons: *Doo wee oo doo.*

All at once, the brassy tone of the alarm in the hallway sounds. We stop all our work, stunned.

"Fire bell. *Go!*" is all the teacher says, propelling us from our desks.

We rise as one and hurry out the door—*no* running— and move as quickly as we can to one of three stairways.

Is it a real fire this time? we wonder. Each of us, our hearts racing, dashes out the classroom door and down the hall in lines, like we are trained to do.

Our feet descend. We are pulled along, sliding our hands over the curves of the polished wooden railing, seeing only the person right in front of us. We patter, placing our feet in the well-worn spots on the wide wooden stairs. We never know until we swing around the stairs on the first floor, whether or not *this* fire is real. We do not know until we pass the fire marshal holding a stopwatch in the downstairs hall. His eyes are fixed on it, not on us. He looks at it intently, with a frown.

The teachers do not tell us we have only one minute to empty the building, one minute for them to move two hundred children down many wooden steps—but we do know that we must get outdoors to line up on the slanted asphalt.

We laugh with relief as we push open the huge wooden door to the outside.

"*Quiet!!!*" our teacher demands, a whispered shout. Quickly, quickly, we form our class lines.

The teacher walks to our line holding her attendance book and begins calling out our names. Sometimes we wait in rain, or snow, for the outside bell, the friendlier bell, to ring and let us back into the school, and when it is not raining, and it's pretty outside, it's okay with the teachers if we move a little slower.

Only a tinderbox, we have heard our families whisper about our school. Dad does not say anything about it. He has stood in his firefighter uniform and watched the children drill. He cannot speak aloud how frightening it all is.

More than any other lesson we will ever learn in our school, is how big the danger is, and the wild fear of it stays with us.

◆ ◆ ◆

There is another memory from first grade that keeps coming back to me.

I am walking the slate sidewalks to school. It is night, and it is raining. All the streetlights are on, and I can see the lights in the houses as I walk past. The colored leaves are pasted to the black, wet slate, and it is slippery to go downhill in our leather shoes in the pouring rain that doesn't seem to end under this night sky. It is raining, and it is hard to breathe.

But now I realize as I look back into this memory it isn't night, after all. It is day. A fog has capped in the smoke of the valley, and day has turned to night. Everything is blurry and dark.

I was home a lot that fall and winter, frequently ill with a cough and infections. I spent my time in bed looking at enormous *Life* magazines from the 1940s, collected and stored in our attic. I couldn't read them. All I could do was turn the pages and look for the very few advertisements colored with ink. The pages were huge and glossy, and beneath their glossy sheen, the paper had yellowed from our poisoned air.

I remember, too, how my firefighter father began collapsing, and all too frequently spent time in the hospital under an oxygen tent. How he was not home very much from all the sickness he experienced.

What I didn't know was that the smoke and the rain enveloped us in sulfuric acid—acid rain. It saturated our air in concentrations that caused paint to peel from houses and cars, and within hours created holes in clothing hung on laundry lines.

Like many families in times of illness, our family was left on its own—although I have to imagine that in our valley of 150,000 people, there were many families believing they had to get through it on their own. No one named the responsibility of the coal producers, because it was understood that the assembled population of immigrants and their progeny was there to run the industry of coal. No one would dare question what sustained our valley. Questioning coal was simply not part of our education.

IV. In Black and White: Lost Images

George Inness's *The Lackawanna Valley* carries a vision of a landscape distilled through the heart and mind of one artist. It is a celebration of progress and industry cutting through an Appalachian spring. Soft pastel colors bring ease to the viewer while one black locomotive puffs through the greenery.

Yet competing with my memory of the sweetness of the Inness painting, there is the shadowy memory of the black-and-white photograph—*the other picture* I remembered seeing in my childhood.

Many years had gone by before I finally found a copy of the photograph in an exhibition catalog of Inness's paintings. The caption read: Scranton, Pennsylvania 1859. A devastating photo clearly taken from the location where George Inness had stood. It outlined the curving shapes of road, roundhouse, and mountains. But instead of tree stumps in the foreground, the black-and-white, silver nitrate-captured, light and shadow image showed grim-looking houses. A river mostly denuded of trees. No boy—no people. No trains. The tracks were there, but no locomotives were in view. In the middle ground were many downtown brick buildings and thick smoke; farther back, poking through the haze, were tall, industrial smokestacks.

———

With the rediscovery of the 1859 image, I crossed over in my understanding. This, I thought, is what the Lackawanna Valley really looked like from George Inness's vantage point. Though Inness painted a mist in the valley, it could not compare with the obscuring smoke shown in the photograph. Much more industry and burning of fossil fuels existed than was displayed in the painting. The photo told the story of a brutal claim on the land.

A decade after Inness painted *The Lackawanna Valley*, in 1866, the city of Scranton was incorporated.

A musical ballad portrays one well-known mine disaster in that decade. It occurred just downriver from where the painting was sketched out. 110 men and boys were buried underground in a single coal mine in Avondale in 1869. The wooden lining of the mine shaft—the only entrance and exit to the mine—caught fire and ignited the breaker building over it. The fire trapped and suffocated the men and boys in the mine. Though it was the largest loss of life in one accident, the Avondale Mine disaster was only one of a string of disasters in the anthracite region, continuing well into the next century. During this same era, young boys hired to scrub the iron smelters also died at an alarming rate. The machinery of coal and rail production was just beginning to go into full swing, pulling immigrants into mines and forges, sacrificing their young men and boys, leaving behind a valley of widows wearing black.

For some in Scranton, the nineteenth century was a time of greatness. The city spread out over the valley floor and up onto the mountain slopes, and the wealthy celebrated their prominence through fabulous architecture. Residential, commercial, and public buildings flaunted riches: ornate, Italianate, Romanesque, a city block of pure Gothic buildings. Less than a century later, those of us born into the past glory of the valley were awed by the monumental downtown remnants of that era: a Gothic high school and library, a Romanesque courthouse and city hall, and the French Renaissance DL&W railroad station with its Tiffany stained-glass atrium and rare Siena marble walls.

The Inness painting was lost over the years, given up by a railroad and its officials who perhaps saw that 1850s locomotive as outdated and no longer an accurate portrait of the railroad's glorious progress. Before Inness's life was over, the DL&W Railroad grew to become a powerhouse, moving steel rails, people, and anthracite coal with forty trains daily, in and out of the Lackawanna Valley. Four competing railroads within the valley vied with the Lackawanna for hauling coal to the nation: Delaware and Hudson, Erie, Northwestern and Ontario, and the Central Railroad of New Jersey. The DL&W focused its attention on "clean-burning" anthracite and created its signature advertising with a new image—that of an elegant woman in a white gown. A new railroad president hired a model to create the persona named *Phoebe Snow*. She was the queen of passenger service on the *Road of Anthracite*. The black diamond anthracite steam locomotives of the DL&W Railroad were purported to give a cleaner ride than their competitors' bituminous burning engines. Phoebe Snow became the symbol of the Lackawanna Railroad. In the clever advertising campaign, the image of the white-gowned lady appeared across the eastern seaboard accompanied by couplets rhyming with *anthracite*.

> *Says Phoebe Snow*
> *About to go*
> *Upon a trip to Buffalo*
> *"My gown stays white*
> *From morn till night*
> *Upon the Road of Anthracite"*
>
> *Phoebe says,*
> *And Phoebe knows*
> *That smoke and cinders*
> *Spoil good clothes*
> *'Tis a pleasure and delight*
> *To take the Road of Anthracite*
>
> *A cosey seat*
> *A dainty treat*
> *Make Phoebe's*
> *Happiness complete*
> *With linen white*
> *And silver bright*
> *Upon the Road of Anthracite...*

The name *Phoebe Snow* remained synonymous with the Lackawanna Railroad and the valley right to the last passenger train in 1966.

—

The original advertising of the DL&W railroad, the commissioned Inness painting, resurfaced in the strangest of circumstances.

The Lackawanna Valley was found in a Mexico City junk shop by none other than George Inness and his wife in 1885, thirty years after he had painted it. It had traveled to Mexico with a load of office furnishings. The shopkeeper valued the gilded frame more than the painting. He knew nothing of its origin or who had painted it and was glad to sell it cheap.

Inness purchased the painting, and as he walked out of the shop, he said to his wife, "Do you remember, Lizzie, how mad I was because they made me paint the name on the engine?"

Growing up in Scranton, Pennsylvania, I always wanted to know our place in the larger history of our country. From my family, from my community, from my teachers in elementary school, I heard how important coal was to the economy and history of our nation. And everywhere I looked, I saw coal in motion—leaving the valley in mile-long coal trains. In school, I was taught that we in the Lackawanna Valley lived in an important place—mighty—powering the nation, and the nation depended upon us.

I read about coal. It seemed imbued with magic: compressed ancient plant material that, like in the fairytale where straw is spun into gold, could bring fabulous wealth. And in one hundred years' time, coal was chemically altered and transformed, spun into products undreamed of in the nineteenth century, to fill consumer shelves: fuels for electricity, pesticides, rubbers, plastics and tars for construction, melamine for dishware, cooking gas for stoves, nylon for clothing and aniline dyes to color it, medicines like sulfa drugs, to save lives; saccharin, aspirin, ink, cosmetics, perfumes, phonograph records, and pencil lead. Coal so infused our lives, it was even a magical toy: my mama had a recipe for growing a crystal garden in a glass dish using coal, ammonia, and food coloring—all derived from coal.

Coal also poisoned our water and air and made us ill. It brought us boom and bust. Growing up in the Lackawanna Valley, I didn't have the ability to name coal as the devil's bargain that it was.

With each history textbook, I pored over in my classroom and in the public library, I searched the index for *Scranton,* or *anthracite,* or *coal.* I wanted to know if we were included—really, officially recognized in books. I was searching for affirmation through images.

In my adulthood, I discovered historic postcard photographs documenting Scranton's glory at the turn of the twentieth century: the grand architecture, scenes of people in voluminous clothing, strolling along the courthouse square promenade or park paths.

The black-and-white photo postcards of the early 1900s were a popular and inexpensive form of communication. In addition to photo postcards of beautiful churches and hotels, black-and-white photos of coal breakers were put on postcards. Some photographers captured the most dismal scenes—miners carried out from underground on stretchers, followed by the members of a community in mourning; the dreary repetition of streets lined with mine-company-owned shacks; crowded houses and collapsed houses; a two-story, brick-façade school, broken, tilted, and pulled into a mine. Haze infused the background of each photo.

One photo that has been reprinted in history books about the anthracite region shows babushka'd women and their children, mine families, picking coal from a towering culm hill; desperate women collecting coal to light a stove and heat soup; women bent down, intent on keeping from slipping and being buried alive by coal.

Other black-and-white photos documented coal's impact on the Lackawanna Valley: the photos of working children from the early twentieth century. Photos of breaker boys, door trappers, spraggers, mule drivers, and miners were secretly caught by the lens of National Child Labor Committee activist, Lewis Hine: children with bodies completely covered in wool clothing and high-laced boots on their feet—with every bit of clothing and skin coated in coal dust, children whose faces show gestures of other lands, and aging unconnected to their young years and small statures. Boys as young as five-years-old who began their work in the breakers and hoped to one day become miners. They worked in coaldust-saturated air, and in winter, it was so cold in the breakers that their lunches would freeze.

In the photographs, some boys smile, some show sass. Some boys are shown scarred, sightless, or have lost limbs. Many boys appear confused or sad. They had snuck away from the bosses for their chance at immortality, these boys who worked the coal to keep the trains running, to feed the steel furnaces, to power the milling of rails that ran the length of the country. Because of Hine's photography work, the movement against child labor was strengthened. Congress passed child-labor laws beginning in 1916, but the struggle for children's dignity ended only in 1938 with the Fair Labor Standards Act of 1938. The child provisions of the FLSA were designed to protect the education of youth and prohibit dangerous employment, and within a few years the national maxim was that no child under sixteen years of age should leave school for gainful employment.

We children who lived in the Lackawanna Valley in the 1950s and 1960s never saw these photos of breaker boys—children like us, but not like us. Though we grew up watching the slow ending of anthracite coal as king, we continued to imagine ourselves as important to our country and our country's history because of the work done in our valley. At one of the many five-and-dime stores downtown, we could purchase color-enhanced lithographed postcard scenes showing an active downtown and cultural life. Oddly, these postcards showing Lackawanna Avenue in the 1940s and 1950s were still available in the 1960s—and newer ones never appeared.

Two decades after child labor laws were put in place, in the 1950s, our family black-and-white photos showed us in our backyards, or posed in the wooden hallways of our nineteenth-century school buildings for class photos. We heard conflicting views of our city from our elders. *If you could play Scranton*—the old adage went—*you could play anywhere.* The saying referred to the discriminating tastes of theatergoers in the city and how they helped determine the future of Broadway plays. Our elders also called our home *The City on Stilts* because the wooden posts in the mines beneath our yards began to rot and collapse the ground on which we lived. We had never owned the ground beneath our houses.

It wasn't bad enough that our valley began emptying of people during the Great Depression and never stopped, or that the land was black while the rivers ran orange. It wasn't enough that smoke rose from the burning piles of waste coal lining the length of the Lackawanna River, and below ground, the mines caught fire. The air we breathed day and night was smoke-filled and reeked of the rotten-egg sulfur smell. The ornate nineteenth-century buildings, our fabulous city architecture, crumbled or mysteriously burned down. Around us everywhere were ill and unemployed miners, machinists, and factory workers. Sanatoriums topped the mountains—refuges for the wealthier members of the community with lung disease to escape the smoke for a while. Twice yearly, the Tuberculosis Society van with its heavy x-ray equipment parked in front of our schools. We children entered it, and one by one splayed our chests on the screen to find out who among us were the next victims.

Anthracite had been so crucial to our nation's economy at the beginning of the twentieth century that striking, unionized minors in Scranton, Pennsylvania in 1902 shut down the nation, and President Theodore Roosevelt had to negotiate to get commerce running again. But when I was growing up in the same city sixty years later, it was Adlai Stevenson whose words were remembered and often quoted. On a presidential campaign stop in Scranton in 1956, he outright called the place "a hellhole."

We of the Lackawanna Valley were defeated.

Searching newer textbooks in the 1970s for *Scranton,* or *anthracite,* or *coal* yielded no entries, and the 1971 World Book spelled it out this way:

> "At one time, the economy of the Scranton region depended solely on coal. But mining has declined…"

Yet, in my heart, the longing for the painting's beautiful landscape lingered.

Gas Stove

There will be no visiting this winter Saturday. Mama won't walk anywhere in slippery winter weather. Warm radiator fragrance mixes with the scents of yeasted dough and damp cloth; Mama is baking bread. A large, old aluminum kettle rests atop an upstairs radiator. A threadbare, brown and ivory blanket swaddles and covers the kettle filled with rising bread dough.

"Mama? Can I paint?"

"Not now," says Mama in answer to my plea for watercolors. "I've got to take care of the dough."

Mama marches upstairs to the bedroom. I follow close behind. Sometimes Mama moves so quickly it's easy to lose sight of her.

"Why don't you put the bread dough on a downstairs radiator?"

"Because it's warmer upstairs. This house is drafty. Cold air always comes in under the doors."

Mama reaches the churring radiator and quickly unwraps the blanket from the aluminum kettle. Carefully she removes the damp piece of cotton sheeting covering the opening. Smells of musty warm cotton are replaced with yeasty smells. After a peek at the dough, Mama wraps her arms around the kettle and quickly heads downstairs to the kitchen table. The bread dough had been making its second attempt to reach the top of the pan, and now Mama catches it and punches it down again. She lifts out the dough and pulls it apart into four small piles. These she gently places into four oiled black loaf pans. She rubs the fleshy tops of the loaves with oil. They look like baby backs.

"Why are you putting oil on their backs?" I ask.

"Their backs?" Mama laughs. "You mean oil on the tops of the loaves? So they don't dry out."

She sets the pans in the oven. Beneath them she sets a broad square pan of hot water. Here the dough will rise one last time, until its rounded top swells above the pan rims.

When the loaves are ready for baking, Mama reaches up behind the stove to the black metal matchbox holder hung on the wall. She picks out a wooden match and strikes it on the rough, black inside rim of the oven door. *Swaahp!* The match's blue tip bursts into orange flame. Mama sets it into a little hole at the bottom of the oven and at the same time turns the center handle. *Whummp!* The gas catches the match's orange flame and turns it blue. In a flash, bright blue flames multiply, outlining the square oven floor. Wells of blue flame hover over an edge of black—like the ghostly blue flames that flicker all over the conical heaps of culm dumps, the mountainous waste piles from coal mining that have caught on fire. At night, for miles and miles along the river flats and railroad tracks, the pointy mountains of blue flames burn. They burn all day, too, but we can't see the flames—just the smoke. By day, the culm dumps are smoking heaps of sad, rusted, pink ash that tower over the nearby houses.

Mama brings the glass tea kettle to the sink to fill it. I follow. She sets the kettle on the back burner and turns the knob. A hiss, then *phhoff!* A serrated circle of blue appears beneath the kettle. I watch the circle's steady flame.

"Mama, do culm dumps have gas?"

Mama walks back to the stove. "It's a coal gas, I guess."

"Mama, is gas 'coal gas'?"

"What are you asking, honey?" Mama crosses her arms against her chest.

"The stove gas. Is that 'coal gas'?"

"No. Some people get *bottled* gas from coal, made at the gas plant downtown. Not us anymore. Our stove has natural gas. We buy it from the Gas and Water Company. It comes in the pipe." She points to the rust-colored pipe at the back of the stove, coming up through the hole in the blue linoleum, bending its iron knee up to reach the stove. "And there's the shut-off knob." She points. "If the pilot light goes out, we have to turn the knob off right away and open windows…we could have an explosion."

My dad's voice rings in my head. I hear my dad saying, *If the pilot light goes out, don't light it. Shut the gas off and open the windows. Never light a match.*

Never! Dad tells me over and over how houses have blown up, houses with moms and kids inside, because someone forgot this. I have seen the gas pipes, mangled and lonely, sticking up out of an ashy pit that was once a house or a downtown store. A fire that Dad fought—and lost. *Gas leaks. Don't forget,* says Dad. *Shut off the gas— don't light a match.*

Though I am afraid of the gas stove, I still think it's pretty. I love the bread that comes from it and the baking times when Mama and I make cakes and pies. At the back of the stove on top, a shelf displays small teapots that Mama keeps for decoration. In the front of the stove there are two oven doors. On the right side of the stove is the gas oven. On the left is another oven, with a narrow door. A secret oven: a coal burning oven that our family doesn't use anymore.

"Can we open the other oven—just to look?"

"The coal stove?" She opens the door to the brick-lined firebox and iron grate. She folds back the enamel cover on top to show me two iron platters and the wire handle for lifting them. "You can cook on these burners when you use it."

I love the coal stove. The old ladies down the street still use theirs—and their kitchens are cozy warm in the fall and winter. A burning coal stove is like a fireplace: you can hear the crackling and see flickering when the door is open. I can pretend we have logs like people long ago.

Mama lifts the glass kettle from the burner and pours hot water over the tea bag in her cup. She lets it rest on the table and goes back to the sink to scrape sticky dough from the aluminum kettle.

"Mama, can we use the coal stove this winter? Mrs. Davis uses hers, and so do the Steigers."

"We don't need it. The new furnace in the basement heats the house."

"But you used it one time…"

"That's because the furnace broke, remember? It was cold that night." Mama nods. "We stayed in the kitchen, and I couldn't even get a fire going with the newspaper and wood."

"But Mama, the coal stove in Mrs. Davis's house makes the kitchen nice."

"I don't want coal or ashes in the kitchen," Mama says as while she rinses the kettle. "There are ashes all over the house from burning the coal in the basement. Ugh. Ashes in the kitchen." Mama shakes her head in disgust. "I have too much to clean without that. No. No more." She dries the pan and pauses. "Besides, we don't even have any Chestnut coal for it. We use Pea size coal."

*Pea coal. Pea coal. Please porridge hot. Pea coal…*I play with the sounds in my mouth. "Why is it called Pea coal?"

Mama reaches for a dishtowel and dries the kettle. "It's the name of that size of coal—the kind we burn in our stoker furnace. A smaller kind. It would fall through this stove grate."

"So why do we burn a smaller kind?"

"Because that's what our furnace takes. Ours is a stoker furnace. It stokes itself from the hopper using smaller coal. Grandma's furnace is an old-fashioned kind. You have to shovel bigger coal in. Chestnut coal."

"Why is Chestnut bigger than Pea Coal?"

"That's just a *name*, honey. The different sizes of coal

have different names. Let's see, there's Egg coal, and Stove coal, and Steam coal—they're really big—as big as my hand. And there's Buckwheat coal—that's really small. That's the kind in my ma's house. I think there's even a kind called Birdseye—as small as a bird's eye, maybe?"

Mama continues, "We can't use the coal stove for cooking. We shouldn't even have tried to light it. There's no pipe to the chimney. We took the pipe away. See?"

She points upward to the top of the chimney to a copper-edged chimney-hole cover that I love looking at. It has a painting in its center circle—the only painting in our house. In it are mountains, bluish in the background like our mountains—only in front there aren't any gray buildings or sidewalks, or Culm dumps. There's a shepherd boy in a straw hat watching sheep in a green and amber field. His staff, rounded on top like a hairpin, is held sideways as he watches. In front of him, the sheep are grazing. You can see bells around their necks. I love this picture. It reminds me of Little Boy Blue in the poem, calling his sheep.

I asked Mama one time where the place was in the painting.

"You mean the picture on the chimney-hole cover? It's made up," she told me.

I look to the painting. I want it to be real. I'm sure it is. I want to walk into that place and look up at the blue sky; I want to feel the breeze and hear the sheep's bells ring and put my hands on their thick woolly coats. I want to see the river there. Our river and our creeks run orange. Maybe their river runs blue.

"Mama, why do we live here?"

Mama shrugs her shoulders sideways, as if to flick off offending notions. She looks downward with a frown, completing the gesture, all this taking place in an instant. "Because we do," she says.

"But why, Mama? Why can't we live out on a farm?"

"Because we don't."

"But why?"

"We just don't." She pauses a moment, and then her voice and pitch rise. "How can you ask such a thing? We were born here—this is where we live." She pauses and looks at me, frowning. She is searching for a clue of how I can be so obtuse.

"Couldn't we move, Mama?"

"Of course not. How would we live?" Mama throws her hands outward. "Where would we get money? How could we leave Grandma behind? Think! Who would take care of her?"

In the evening, a loaf of fresh-baked bread rests on the table, and other loaves fill the breadbox. Dad has come home after four days at the fire station. He sits in front of the TV, polishing his shoes. With a small round brush, he buffs and buffs his dress shoes the way he learned to do in the war, making the shoes into black mirrors.

On the TV screen, there's a picture of a happy family in pretty clothes in a modern house, and then there's the picture of a flame. It looks like the blue flame on the poster at the Gas and Water office where Mama pays the bill. The words on the ad read, *gas* and *cleaner* for heating houses. As much as I like the idea of a crackling fire in the coal stove in the kitchen, I like the idea of "clean heat" even more. Maybe we could get a gas furnace, and we'd be like the family on TV. I want to be like that family.

"Why don't we get gas?" I ask Mama and Dad.

"What do you mean?" Mama shakes her head.

"Why don't we get gas like other people do to heat the house?"

"Who heats their houses with gas?" Mama asks.

"People who have more money than we do," Dad answers, shaking his head.

"Look at where we live," Mama says. "We mine coal. We use coal." She says it as if it's a pact we've made, those of us living in this place.

"But on the TV they said gas is *cleaner* heat. You don't like coal or coal dust."

"We don't mine natural gas in our mountains," says Dad. "It's cheaper to use coal. Besides, we would have to get a new furnace and heating system."

"Dad, what about *coal gas*? There is gas from coal…"

"You mean *bottled gas*. It's natural gas that was made from coal at the gas plant downtown. We don't use that anymore. Our gas comes in the pipe. *Coal gas* is different. It's a poisonous gas that comes from burning coal." He packs his shoe brushes back into the wooden box. "You can't smell it. That's why people die sometimes in their sleep."

Coal gas got Grandma's next-door neighbor, an old woman, and dad had to run there with another firefighter to revive her. "Grandma keeps her bedroom window open at night, right?"

"Just a crack," Dad replies. He shakes his head and has a strange smile on his face. "Of course, our window-panes are so loose we get air at night anyway, don't we?" He looks at me. "You don't have to worry about it. The furnace and coal are in the basement, and you sleep two stories above it, so you can't get hurt."

On the black-and-white screen of the TV set, the June Taylor Dancers are making flowery circle patterns on their black and white stage. I'm distracted and lost in another image: a flame and its promise. The idea of clean heat lingers for me. I'd like to live the way they do on television— clean, with new clothes and shoes, and natural gas in the furnace. No shovels, no ashes, no coal gas creeping up the stairs at night.

As we watch TV, the coal furnace rumbles and crunches beneath our living room floor. When all is still, when we're upstairs lying on our beds, we'll hear coal trains rumble upgrade. We know who we are. It's our coal on those trains. *Our coal.* Our fuel to burn.

Dioramas

The afternoon in Nay Aug Park is unbearably hot; being in the pool so long makes me tired, and I'm not ready for the long walk home. When we reach the shade trees in the park behind the Everhart Museum, I ask, "Can we go in?"

"To the museum? Okay. Only for a little while."

We climb the stone steps to the heavy front doors, lean back and pull to enter a delicious coolness. I feel such happiness walking the white terrazzo floor in the quiet lobby. The hush of the museum falls over us—a hush of importance—different from church hush or library hush. And unlike the lobbies of downtown buildings, the museum is clean and filled with light.

"Where do you want to go?" Mama asks

I lead her to the place where we always start: a small hall right near the entry. Glass cases on the floor display slabs of coal and coal fossils bigger than dinner plates. The walls are decorated with paintings of scaly trees topped with fronds. The trees overlook a tangle of ferny greenery through which huge dragonflies soar. The dragonflies are beautiful but frightening because they're so big. The trees look odd because they don't have normal branches.

"Those trees look so strange."

"They're from a long time ago. Tree ferns."

We look at the different kinds of coal: lignite, bituminous, and anthracite, and huge slabs of coal with shiny black fossil imprints of leaves, and sometimes ridges that look like tire tracks.

"Where do the fossils come from?"

"I don't know—probably from a mine."

As we leave the hall, we pass a sculpture of a coal miner carved from anthracite. Beneath his helmet and headlamp, his face is etched with deep lines.

"Coal art," Mama says, shaking her head. "So strange. Why would anyone do that?"

I look at his face. It's drawn and hollowed out. He looks like the men we see everywhere.

Mama takes me to the basement to look at exhibits of minerals, and the exhibit of living bees. Their buzzing bodies cover a wax comb sandwiched between two layers of glass that vibrate. A river of honeybees fills a glass tube that leads outdoors, but it is a two-way river, with bees heading out and crawling over returning sisters. The honeybee exhibit is the only part of the Everhart that has something living. The bee tube is a tunnel like a mine— only it's bees, and they don't mine coal. They mine nectar—or maybe sunshine.

On the second floor, we look at artwork—paintings of people and places in our valley long ago. We sigh over the beautiful collection of Dorflinger and Tiffany cut glass that was made in furnaces in a neighboring valley, and which graced the tables of the very wealthy. Oh, how I love the sparkles of light on the cut glass. I wish my family had them on fancy tables—maybe then we could dress up at the table and have maids like in the stories in books.

Mama and I go back downstairs to a black-walled room. A bench faces a wall glass case where large rocks are displayed in tiers. Mama lets me touch a switch on the exhibit, and the lights in the glass case turn on. Then the lights in the room go out except for an ultraviolet light over the rocks. The crusty fluorescent coatings on the rocks glow strange, bright colors: pink, purple, green—colors we never see anywhere else—not in our clothing, not even in the brightest flowers or in paintings. The plain room lights come back on. We touch the switch again and watch the colors change and change back.

"Come on," says Mama.

"Please, Mama, just one more time." I am drawn to the strangeness and the beauty of the colors, and each time the regular case lights come on, I try to see where the hidden colors live on the rocks, but I can't. Before I can memorize the patterns, the lights change again. Mama doesn't understand that I want to see them so I can look for rocks like these on our mountain.

"One more time?"

"Let's go see the bird room." Mama heads out.

We pass through a room of wild animals and mounted heads that neither of us likes so that we can get to the bird room. Rows and rows of glass and dark, stained wood cabinets taller than us fill the room. Mama lets me wander as I wish, and I visit the large dioramas set in each of the room's four corners.

Each is a window into a different wilderness landscape. I am drawn to the marshland scene, where redwinged blackbirds cling atop painstakingly puffed-out cattails. The red and yellow patches on the blackbirds' wings sing out over the amber colors in the exhibit case. I wish I could climb right into the diorama, right into the autumn landscape. I go find Mama among the cabinets and bring her to the diorama.

"Mama, where is that?"

"It says 'Pennsylvania Marsh.'"

"Could we find one?"

"Find one what?"

"A place like it."

Mama considers this for a moment. "It would be by water…a pond or something." She shakes her head. "There'd only be water like that in the Flats by the river. The culm dumps are in the Flats by the river. That's where the collieries and breakers are. No cattails there." She holds out her hand. "Come on."

We wander between cabinets of hundreds of birds, of all sizes and colors, mounted on perches and labeled— including strange ones that have been brought from across the world: the bird of paradise with huge plumes, gulls, and long-legged water birds that would never be found in our mountains. We look at the many sizes of owls with their flat faces. They're all organized by groups and kinds.

"They're real, right, Mama?"

"They're real, but they're not alive. Those are real feathers, but the eyes are made of glass."

Mama goes around a case and calls to me. "Come see this one," she says.

Mama stands before a dove-like bird, with a fabulous, long, jewel-colored teal and maroon tail. His glass eyes, encircled by tiny white rings, make him seem sweet.

"*Passenger Pigeon*," Mama reads to me from the card in the glass case. "They're all gone," she says quietly. "We won't ever see them again. They told us in school. They've gone extinct."

"Why?"

"I don't know. I think they were shot. Hunted."

Mama frowns and looks downward, searching for answers. "For food maybe? I can't remember. It's a terrible loss."

"But...can't we find one in the woods?"

"They're gone."

On the way out of the museum, we pass the coal fossils. Fern trees. Extinct. Giant dragonflies. Extinct. Like dinosaurs. Like the coal-burning steam locomotives that used to run all through the valley that I never got to see. Gone.

Back outdoors, we walk behind the museum, among trees, and past an 1850s railway car sitting on a short set of rails: a passenger car from the time of the gravity railroads, the first railroads to move coal. There's a mine, too, in the other part of the park, by the black rocks below the picnic area, a place we don't go to very much.

"Mama, can we go see the mine?"

"The Brooks Mine?" Mama hesitates before answering. "I don't know if it's open."

"*Please*, Mama."

We walk to the picnic grounds and come to a tunnel opening set in a wall of layered black rock. The iron gates are swung away from the entrance. Mama and I walk down the coal-covered path holding hands. We step just inside the entrance and are met with a cold draft of bitter coal-odored air. Mama stops and listens to see if anyone else is inside. I begin shivering.

"We can't go in there alone," she says. "We'll wait until your dad can come with us."

Dad comes with us to the park on a rare summer Sunday when his rotating firefighting schedule gives him a break. Because we are with him, we go to the park by car. Mama and Dad dress up as if are going to the next town to visit relatives—Dad in a short-sleeved, button-down shirt and he even wears Brylcreem in his hair. Mama puts on one of her flowered, full dresses, and has pulled back her graying curls to show her pearly clip-on earrings. They let me wear shorts. On Sundays, the park is full of families with their dads, instead of just mamas and kids. The day feels so special with the three of us together—just like other families.

Mama, Dad, and I walk down the path to the mine's dark opening. It's set right into the tilted coal layers that lie below the picnic area.

"Is this a real coal mine?"

"No, it's just for looking," Dad answers.

Hand in hand, we enter and walk between a set of rails. Though a dim trail of caged light bulbs overhead guide the way, the tunnel slopes gradually, curving, pulling us into darkness. There's a heaviness and a chill. We do not speak. The only sounds in the mine are our footsteps crunching on coal, echoing, and water dripping somewhere. We travel downslope, hesitating. We listen for something—other people visiting—or maybe creatures. Perhaps rats. The darkness thickens. For a few moments, we can't see what is ahead or behind us. I squeeze my parents' hands, and they squeeze back gently to let me know they're paying attention.

Ahead in the yellowish light, we see an eerie scene: in an alcove, two mannequins stand in miners' helmets and clothing. A man and a boy. They stand beside a shaggy mule attached to a massive wooden coal cart filled with huge chunks of anthracite. Leaning against the coal cart are tools: pickax, shovel, and lantern.

I look at the coal cart, but I am afraid to look up at the mannequins. They are so very different from mannequins in a downtown store window—they look more like people who froze in place. Their clothing is filthy, and shaggy hair peeks out from beneath the miner's helmets. Smudges of coal dust mark their faces. The yellowed light casts a brownish gleam on the walls of coal around them.

For a few moments, we are silent, as if we have approached some kind of altar, where statues of saints in alcoves would look peacefully out at us. But this is dark and creepy. Even in the dim light I can see that the mule is missing patches of hair. The boy's clothes are dirty and torn. I can't take my eyes off him.

I whisper to my parents, "Why is there a boy in here?"

Dad answers. "Boys worked in mines. They took care of mules."

"Are there still boys in mines?"

"No, not anymore."

"C'mere." Dad takes my hand and leads me beyond the mannequins to a room carved from the coal, off to the right. We face a huge pillar carved of coal. Dad takes me on the dimly lit pathway around the pillar, walking quickly. The mine floor tilts crazily downward. Following the narrow curving path with only coal walls on either side of us, we feel as if we are on some strange amusement park ride. Then the floor gradually tilts back up as we reach the miner mannequins. Mama waits for us, her arms tightly crossed. She quickly takes my hand. We talk in whispers as we head out of the tunnel, our steps quicker than when we came in.

"Are there still people in a mine?"

"Yep, there are miners."

"Do they stay in the mines?"

"They live in houses. But there aren't so many miners as there used to be."

"Why not?"

"Well, there aren't so many mines as there used to be. Not everyone heats with coal anymore."

In the distance, we can hear the muffled echoes of other families, and it sounds strange to hear people again.

At the mine's opening, we enter back into the summer day, blinking at the sunlight, breathing warm summer air, feeling as if we've gone on a very long journey.

East Mountain

East Mountain, which rises up above our hollow, is my dad's special place. His aunts, uncles, and cousins live up there in the woods, separated from us by the steep slope and the railroad tracks. At the top is Mountain Lake—that's where our creek down at the bottom of our hollow comes from. East Mountain is the highest place that Mama and I can walk. At the bottom of the valley and downtown is the Headquarters fire station. My dad is part of both places.

When Mama and I want a special adventure, we walk up the mountain to visit relatives, but we never go up to the top where the lake is. Mama is afraid to go some places alone with me, so we only go there when Dad takes us.

Dad doesn't walk as much as me and Mama. That's how we get around. Dad usually drives to work at the fire station headquarters downtown, in the valley, or to Grandma's house three blocks away. I guess it's because of his asthma—or maybe because he doesn't have the kind of time Mama and I do, because he has to be at work in the day or night, and he's tired a lot.

Mama told me Dad's going to work on the mountain at the fire station there. It's good because he'll be able to breathe better at that station instead of being downtown, at the bottom of the valley, where the smoke is thicker. I know he'll like working on the mountain.

At school, the kids find out my dad's a fireman, and they get all excited.

"Your dad's a fireman?!"

"Nah. You're making it up."

I just shake my head and walk away. I wonder if they would be excited if I said my dad was a miner or factory worker. Is it because fires and sirens get us excited or is it because the firemen in dress uniform get to be in parades? Or is it because at our school's fire drills we're timed by the firefighter who holds the stopwatch? The firefighters are the ones who decide if we we're good enough at getting out of disaster—and how many of us they can save if disaster comes.

My dad does drive a fire truck. He can even drive the ambulance. He times the fire drills. He leaves home any time there's a general alarm blaze downtown. He sets up hoses, climbs ladders, and wrestles with the impossible canvas snake hose. He tries to put fires out. Dad knows how to help someone with first aid. He can wrap a burn or get a heart started again.

Once he rescued a worker who had fallen inside an empty gas tank at the anthracite gasworks downtown. Dad and another firefighter carried a stretcher up a ladder into the tank and brought the unconscious man out. My uncle boasts that the tank was sixty-five feet high—I guess that's higher than our house. No one says whether the man woke up, but it was a dangerous rescue.

I don't think he knows what to do with the loss of the

people who don't make it, though. I think they haunt him, and sometimes I think he still thinks about the ones who didn't make it in the war he was in.

I don't think he likes being around fire, or fireworks either, and neither do I.

One time, on a July night, Mama, Dad, and I went up the mountain to watch the fireworks shoot off. We could have watched it from our back porch, but Dad was there to make sure no fires started in the woods. We were close to the fuses, close to the rocketing fireworks, and the *ffuff-fuff* sound of each one heading skyward. I looked up and saw, instead of fireworks, the grown-ups above me like a forest of dark shapes, the forest of trees layered above them, their faces lit as each fuse flared.

The fireworks burst open. Boom. Boom. I plugged my ears. Whistling. Streaks, boom and *Whap*—something hit the top of my head and bounced. I felt pain. I looked down and see a glowing cinder. I was hit by a cinder. I looked up to Mama. Her hair was pulled back and I could see the glow in the white streaks of hair at her temples and the sparkle in her large, pearly-centered, rhinestone clip-on earrings. She was looking up and happy. And then I looked to Dad. His face in the glow of the light bursts. He looked strange. Or as if he was far away from us—maybe far away inside himself again.

Firefighting means that Dad spends a lot of time away from us. But now that he's going to be on East Mountain, he'll be closer to us.

One day, that's where Dad takes me—to the top of East Mountain.

"Want to go up to Mountain Lake with me?" Dad says, and he hands me a bamboo fishing pole just my size.

We sit on the layers of gray rocks that look like books turned to stone. Dad knows a lot about hunting and fishing and the woods.

The water is silvery and clear, and no fish come.

Dad takes my hand, and we walk the trail along the lake and into the woods.

Dad reaches up to one of the saplings along the trail and slices a birch twig with his pocket knife. He hands me a narrow, bendable twig of the prettiest yellow-brown: shiny, bright, and prettier than any milk chocolate I've ever seen. With his thumb, he pushes back the tissue-paper-thin bark and shows me a bright green wand—the naked twig. He cuts off two pieces the length of bubblegum and hands one to me.

"Here. Put it in your mouth, and chew on it."

Dad puts the other piece into his mouth and smiles. The twig is the flavor of my favorite gum—it's wintergreen.

"Sweet Birch," he says. "It's like candy."

It tastes like a mountain lake. A time away from fire stations.

Dad holds me through bee stings and cheers thunderstorms with me, but I like best that he gives me birch tree candy. I decide then that I want to be able to find every Sweet Birch tree on the mountain and know all the trees in the woods and on our streets.

BRIDGE TO NOWHERE

If the weavers, the women in the huge Scranton Lace factory, could work iron, they would create this: a bridge of lace spun out over the rails and water, reaching from the tilted, coal-laden rocks on one side of the gorge to the other. Hidden from all the houses on the hillsides, the bridge stretches out from the city park and arches over train tunnels to connect to an amusement park across the way—except the park on the other side is a ghost, spun from my grandma's stories of wooden swan boats and arches hung with strings of electric lights. And though I heard the name—Luna Park—and that Grandma remembers it, I cannot understand the bridge. Fire gobbled the park to ash almost fifty years ago, in 1916, when my parents were babies. My family says it's sad that Luna Park is gone. Like a lot of things. But the bridge is still here—a sad bridge—and the strange part is that it doesn't lead to anywhere. There are no houses, no shops, no cemetery on the other side. This bridge goes nowhere except to the other side— just an empty, scrubby, rocky other side.

Long ago, my family says, our city, Scranton, was famous. Coal. Iron. Railroads. But lots of the city has burned down—and some keeps burning. Fires in fancy downtown stores. Fires in the coal mines beneath our streets and houses. Fires on the mountains of coal waste, the culm dumps. Hazes hang over most of the city—except here. The park in the gorge doesn't have fire. It has water over black rock.

Dad brings me to the Bridge to Nowhere, and because he brings me here, I know there's something he loves about it—maybe because it leads to the other end of the mountain above where we live, a side of it we can't get to by walking or driving.

Dad holds my small hand tightly in his thick, muscular one. "Come see," he says, smiling, and I want to cross because I am with him, but this bridge is crumbling pavement suspended by iron lace, fragile enough to shake with our steps. Holes in the asphalt at my feet, like peek-holes, force me to see down, way down, through empty space to the treetops below. To the train tracks. To the brook. Holes smaller, but just as terrifying as the holes that open up in my bedroom floor each night when the radiator hisses. I know a hole will open here when Dad least expects it, and I will fall through. I crowd against his knee and lean against his hand as he takes me out. There is no land beneath us. Halfway across I freeze. I don't want to see the forgotten place.

Cemetery

"It's a beautiful day for a walk. Let's go to the cemetery," Mama says as she heads out the door.

We walk down to the alley that follows our creek through the hollow. The sun is high overhead and trees are dripping green. We pass old people on their porches and fruit trees in tiny, fenced yards. Along the way we cross all the tree streets through our neighborhood: Willow, Birch, Beech, Maple, Elm, Locust. We play a game—we try to find as many as we can of the tree leaves named by the streets.

"Here's a maple leaf!"

"And here's a maple leaf."

"And another, and another and another…"

We laugh.

We reach the last street in our hollow that has a sign: Cherry. "We'll probably find some chokecherry trees near the cemetery," Mama says.

"There's supposed to be Pear Street, right, Mama? What comes after Pear?

"Uh, is it Fig?"

"Pear, Fig. But there aren't any streets here at all. So there really isn't a Pear Street."

"Well, there is, but you can't get to it from here because of the brook and the tracks and the mountainside. It's father down toward the river," Mama pants. "We have no way of getting there from here."

We pass the last house in our hollow and reach the place where our creek empties into the Stafford-Meadow Brook that heads down to the Lackawanna River. Here the road ends, and crumbled pavement leads to the plank bridge over the brook which we must cross to get to our Catholic cemetery. At the sight of the bridge, the fear begins crawling up my belly.

We make our way onto the bridge. There is no sidewalk. The creosoted boards are broad and heavy. Through gaps between the boards, I see the rushing brook below. I close my eyes and hold my breath. I grip Mama's hand. She shakes her head in exasperation.

"Come on. You're acting silly," says Mama as I cling to her hand. "Cars go over this all the time."

"But Mama, the boards move."

Mama just doesn't understand. The bridge rattles any time a car drives over. Planks shift and tip as we go across. When Dad drives across, he grips the wheel and leans forward just a little. I hold my breath and hope we won't go down. Sometimes there are missing planks. Sometimes the bridge is closed.

We cross the bridge and land on the cindered road between the brook and the iron cemetery gate, and walk upstream to the entrance around the bend. The summer sun is high in the sky and thrushes sing. We are alone.

"It's so peaceful here," Mama says. We enter through the gate, and head uphill towards the back fence, walking between speckled gray headstones. "Be careful. You walk along the grave—you can't step on it."

"Yes, Mama, I know."

At most of the graves there is a small American flag waving its red, white, and blue against the green of the cemetery lawn. Potted red geraniums from Decoration Day are still blooming at the headstones.

Among the larger, speckled family headstones, small clusters of white slabs lie on the ground, marking the children's graves. The engraving on the stones is eroded, making them hard to read.

Mama looks at me looking at the stones. "It's sad, isn't it? Some of these children only lived for a few days."

I nod and Mama takes me to my uncle's grave. Now we stand and say a prayer. Next to my uncle's name on the headstone is Grandma's.

"Why is Grandma's name on here?"

"Because she'll be buried here someday."

"Soon?"

"We hope not, but we don't know."

"Mama, can we go see the angel?"

We walk up the hill to see her. Along the way I stop at a few of the graves where old photos are pasted behind yellowed cellophane. The portraits are of people long ago—

men with mustaches and high collars, women with tightly coiled long hair.

The white angel statue holds her hands together in prayer. She's beautiful, and I wish I could talk to her. Mama looks around.

"Mama, can we see the other grave…"

Mama nods. Mama and I walk farther up the hill to read the name of the grandfather I never knew, buried alongside his brother.

"Did you know him, Mama?"

"No, he died during the war, before I met your dad."

"Mama, why isn't your family here?"

"Because I didn't grow up in this neighborhood. Come on. Let's get some water for the flowers before we leave."

As we cross back over the plank bridge, I close my eyes once again.

Mama lifts her head. "Can you smell that? There's something blooming. Let's go see what it is."

Mama and I turn from the main road and walk a cindered alley toward the rail line. The trees line it thickly on both sides. All along the ground we see large, frilly, white snapdragon-ish blossoms.

"Catalpa trees," says Mama with a smile. "Look." She points to the huge heart-shaped leaves. "It's a good shade tree." Mama smiles. "Auntie and I used to make necklaces out of the flowers."

We pick up the fragrant blossoms, capping our fingers with them, and we play with them as we walk back out to the road.

"Mama, is there a Catalpa Street?"

"No. Not that I know of. There's Poplar, Ash, Walnut... even Chestnut. There used to be chestnut trees," Mama shakes her head sadly. "We used to go down to the Corners," she says, talking about the crossroads in her small town. "We'd buy roasted chestnuts—there'd be chestnut roasters on the street, and you could buy roasted chestnuts in a bag. Mmm, they were so good...warm...but there aren't any chestnuts now."

"But your Mama cooks chestnuts."

"My Ma boils the dried chestnuts. The ones from Italy. The American chestnuts—they're gone." Mama looks up as if she's searching for something and then she shakes her hands, palms up. "The trees died. There was some kind of virus that came from a botanical garden when there were these big chestnut trees on the streets—and they just died and looked like great big skeletons. When I was little there were still chestnut trees on the streets. Oh, those trees were so pretty! And the wood from them was gorgeous."

Mama looks up and begins:

Under a spreading chestnut tree
The village smithy stands;
The smith, a mighty man is he,
with large and sinewy hands;
And the muscles of his brawny arms
Are strong as iron bands.

"I had to recite that in school. Was it "The Village Blacksmith"? That was a long time ago, and I still remember it."

"But Mama, where did all the chestnut roasters go?"

"I don't know, honey. It's like that with a lot of things."

Charcoal and Ice

Over time, our city's glory begins to disappear. Though coal is still everywhere, and is always burning, there are other fires, too...five-alarm blazes...eight-alarm blazes... general alarms. Gas explosion...electrical wiring problem...cause unknown. Unknown. Unknown, but another downtown building is now a gap in a row of decrepit brick buildings, windows vacant and dark, like the stares of old miners. The gaps are boarded up with gray-painted plywood mounted at the sidewalk. The demolition crews cut holes into the plywood to give us a peep show, an exhibit of loss: pits filled with bricks and twisted pipes, and the robin's egg blue of a stairwell leaves its imprint on one side of a remaining wall. Looking down from our sidewalk cliff, we see rocks and ashes, broken bricks, dust, and glass shards. Stores are never rebuilt. The holes remain for a long time—season after season—before they're filled in. In winter, icicles hang on charred beams and blackened pipes.

The firefighters are kept busy. Another and another building burns. The loss of businesses to mysterious fires and explosions accelerates, and the shells of buildings are left standing over us, charred and boarded up for years. Perhaps it took a long time for the insurance check to come through—but the owner is long gone, moved away to where business is better. We heave a collective sigh. No more plate glass windows to peer into. No more men's hats to admire. A restaurant gone, a bank, a women's apparel store that had high-class clerks, speaking with the affected diction of 1930s radio chic.

The downtown stores which haven't burned begin to empty, and businesses disappear. Furniture stores, shoe stores, a pharmacy, movie theaters that once housed vaudeville acts. The bus system breaks down after a strike, and the bus lines change. Buses run less often, especially in the evenings, and the downtown department stores stay open less and less at night. Though the Great Depression thirty years earlier had a tremendous impact on the valley's commerce, the never-recovered loss becomes noticeable all at once in the 1960s, and downtown Scranton becomes a ghost town. It begins with burning.

And always there are minefires.

It isn't enough that there is always a smoke and sulfur smell everywhere, from coal burning in each house, factory, or electrical station—it isn't enough that hundreds of culm dumps, five stories high, burn day and night—but there are even fires underground. The fires in the mines rage beneath us.

Living in the Lackawanna Valley, we accept that mines tunnel beneath us and our homes. It's our landscape, and we know that none of us own the mineral rights beneath our yards or houses—that was agreed upon before any of us were born. And that coal companies could and did take more of the coal and rock beneath our city than was legal—that was also something those of us living in the valley accept with a shrug.

The coal companies were greedy. (We never say miners, or accountants, or business owners.) The coal companies took away more coal than any resident ever agreed upon with any greedy politicians. Instead of four-foot by four-foot pillars of coal left in place to support the roofs of the mines and all the land above the mines, they simply left wooden pillars—as if telephone poles could hold the world together, as if logs could do the work of Atlas—as if wooden posts never decay in damp mines.

So, we tilt. We cave in. More and more, we have mysterious seeps, and then, minefires: underground fires whose gases and smoke rise from cracks in city streets downtown, on the side of the town called Minooka, and all the way up the twenty-four miles of the Lackawanna River valley from Old Forge to Carbondale. And since no one knows how the seams of coal and all the hastily and ferociously created hundred-year-old tunnelways connect to one another, we sit stunned and worried.

This is what the end of the world looks like—fires above and below ground. Smoke. Charcoal and ice.

Starlings and pigeons come, gathering in huge flocks atop grimy downtown buildings. Birds line the edges and decorate the rooflines. They must feast on something in the empty buildings because their numbers rapidly increase. As dusk comes and the sun has slipped beyond the blue mountain edge, their shrieks deafen pedestrians.

The city fights back with bird sirens: eerie descending

whistles and gunshot bangs played from loudspeakers atop downtown buildings.

♦ ♦ ♦

Mama and I still go downtown in the dusk of a December evening for Christmas shopping. There's nowhere else to go—and even if there was, we can only go where the buses or our feet can take us. Mama and I join the shoppers who huddle in woolen coats, pull up our collars to hide from the sounds of the whistles and bangs from loudspeakers. We shudder as the flocks rise into the air and land back on the buildings.

Downtown is dying. We rush through our shopping, uneasy, knowing we must hurry past the many dark and empty buildings to catch a bus before buses stop running for the night.

Rattling, chugging, waiting to take that last climb out of the valley, the two-tone green buses look like long beetles racing downtown streets, racing to make their last runs. They deposit their riders home to dark streets and slate sidewalks, speckled by streetlamp light shattered by windy branches.

Mama and I wait for the bus in front of the Globe Store, pushing close to the curb as the buses arrive. Sometimes people in the crowd let Mama and me go first because she has a child. This evening we are all anxious to get away from downtown, and many fill the wide sidewalk between department store and street. Mama and I try to spot buses from the back of the crowd.

A bus arrives with the wrong name for this stop. *Green*

Ridge? That's the wrong direction, we scoff, until the bus driver jumps from his seat. He cranks the paper roll of names, but the paper sign jams. The driver shrugs and sits back down. A roulette. We rush to the nameless bus, hoping the half letters spell out *East Mountain*, the bus we need. We have to ask, "What bus is this?" The driver answers the first in line and we mumble it back through. It is our bus, but we will ride it nameless. We will ride a bus with half names on beige paper, names suspended. It's our only way home at night.

The bus driver swings the doors open hard. The crowd of woolen coats and silk babushkas pushes forward. Mama holds me back, waiting to fit through the door with me on one side and the paper shopping bag on the other. We are among the last to board and we must climb onto the bus quickly for this last ride. Mama pulls me up the steep steps. We watch the impatient driver snatch transfers. Mama sends our coins clinking through the chrome funnel mouth. We move down the aisle as quickly as the crowd will allow, for as soon as we do, the driver swings the accordion doors shut so hard, the black rubber edges bounce in vibration.

We shuffle to the middle of the bus where we latch onto chrome poles. With people in front and behind us in the aisle, I cannot see anything but the floor or ceiling. Paper signs bend above us, following the curve of the roof. Advertising from cigarette packs and safety warnings line the ceiling in irregular racing stripes. The corrugated rubber floor mats below our feet are caked with gum, tar, and spit. Mama is always careful not to set anything down on the bus floor. With one hand Mama holds me against her and with her other hand she steadies herself, holding onto the chrome bar, dark green paper shopping bag handles cutting into her wrist, dangling.

We sway with the wild swings the driver makes into traffic, past all the sad, dark, downtown buildings and the abandoned rails behind them. Up over the bridge and tracks, up, up, out of the valley we climb. We splay our feet as the bus climbs the steep street, tilting us. Passengers disembark into the darkness along the way, and finally, a double seat opens for me and Mama. The green vinyl seats are worn and cracking, split open like seedpods, spewing straw. We sit uncomfortably and I lean against Mama to rest.

Mama nudges me awake, pulls me by the arm up the aisle and out into the night, beneath the streetlamp at Pete's corner store. The bus pulls away quickly, leaving us in oily black smoke. I glance once more to the valley. I cannot see but imagine the dark silhouettes of West Mountain edges across the valley. Down below the rattling goes on all night—the screeching, banging of metal couplers, the roaring rattle of coal being loaded into gondola cars. The smoke of culm dumps rises high on a cold night. Across the street at St. Mary's Hospital, patients cry or sigh in their dreams, sleep in tents of oxygen, gasping for air.

Mama and I wrap our coats tighter as we turn and go downhill to our home in the hollow.

Walking

Mama and I are walking. The rich, summer green has drained from the valley, leaving behind brilliant hues. Mama picks up red maple leaves that have fallen on the dark gray slate sidewalk.

"You see how pretty they are?" she asks me.

Swathed across the tulip-shaped leaves are diagonal and speckled bands of flaming orange, magenta pink, and pale green yellows. Mama wants me to notice the passing colors, just like calling my attention to brilliant sunsets each day at this time of year. The autumn leaves are like the sunsets: vibrant. We walk slowly, searching the sidewalks, filling our hands with bouquets of leaves, and head homeward, happy to press them between layers of waxed paper. We hang them on the windows, trying to hold onto a little bit of color, but the wax is only a small delay in their decay. Over time they wither, too, crumbling into winter.

Mama and I are walking to a garment mill near the bridge to downtown. Mama steps inside the tall, white factory building and leaves me to stand outside the door. From the narrow slate sidewalk, I can see across the gorge to the beautiful DL&W railroad station. Passenger trains pause as coal trains fly past them, beginning the long, steep ascent from the Lackawanna Valley. Between them and where I stand, the Spruce Street Bridge is suspended over rails and water, visibly shaking when cars and buses rumble across it. In school we learned that the iron mills used to be down below by the water, underneath where the bridge is now. The thrumming trains with their heavy loads and the rumbling and creaking of the bridge reverberate through me.

Mama returns with a big cardboard box filled with rags. The leftover mill fabric from the making of the summer cotton dresses will give us and Grandma material for crocheting rag rugs. We'll rip the rags apart and make something new, and Mama is flushed with excitement. Between us we will carry the heavy box one impossible, steep mile back up the mountain. It is hard work. We struggle together, Mama letting us rest every half block or so. Near the top, I can no longer do it. Mama takes the box and wraps her arms all the way around it, carrying it by herself.

We are walking in the rain, Mama and I, close together under a big black umbrella, our navy blue, wet wool overcoats smelling sharply of coal dye. The rains are cold. The large umbrella doesn't cover both of us as we descend into the valley to church. It rocks as Mama walks. We pull our heads down, tip the umbrella forward to keep the cold rain from our heads and eyebrows. The shiny black sidewalks are slippery beneath the smooth leather soles of our pointed shoes, but we trudge dutifully onward.

—

`

Mama and I are together; we walk. I tire from all the steep hills we climb and so often wish we could go by car. I ask her about it all the time.

"Why don't you drive, Mama?"

"I don't need to drive. I can walk. Women aren't supposed to drive cars."

"Why not?"

"Why should women drive cars? They don't need to go anywhere. They need to stay home and take care of their houses."

"But Mama, we don't always stay home."

"Oh…we go to town sometimes, or to my Ma's house. But we can walk or take the bus. Besides, we can't afford a car."

"My teachers drive."

"Well, yeah. But they're different. They have jobs to go to. My job is home."

Mama and I are walking. We walk up the mountain road, stopping at the houses of Dad's uncles, aunts, and cousins scattered across the mountain from one bend in the road to the next. Along the way, we listen to the litany of aches and pains of the elderly relatives and share a cup of tea. We walk to the mountain top where we hug Dad at the fire station, then circle back down the other side of the mountain, visiting more relations.

Mama and I are walking down our backyard to the lower alley to collect wild blackberries. We dive into the brambles and emerge covered with scratches and holding small, sour berries. We take them home, sprinkle on sugar, pour milk over them, and eat like princesses.

We are walking to buses, away from buses, and through Mama's hometown. We are walking to downtown to stand in enormous, ornate vestibules, paying bills at counters designed and built for a past century. Mama and I are walking to run errands, to buy groceries, to window-shop, or to get outside. We know the chip in each slate sidewalk we traverse, we know each hedge. We walk over bridges, rails, and creeks, seeking and telling stories.

Mama and I are walking. I must reach my hand up to hold onto hers—needing her help to go against gravity as we climb steep hills home, as we climb steep stone stairs to church, as we climb up steep stairs to our house and each of the houses we visit. I lean on her hand as we climb many flights of stairs in the hospital to visit our relations. Afterward, we climb to the chapel at the very top of the hospital to light candles for them, and for us.

We are walking, Mama and I, up the hill to the hospital. It must be winter because the hospital has the scent now of a million clothes irons heating at full blast. We climb the metal stairs. I can barely hold on to the shiny, brown-painted rail, but I pull and pull up three-and-one-half tall hospital flights to the landing. Mama leaves me at the landing window while she slips through the metal door. I cannot see through the meshed glass window so high up in the door, so I look out at the valley, seeing so many house lights, streetlamps, and factory windows all the way down to the bottom of the darkened slope. In a few minutes, Dad slips through the doorway to the landing. He is dressed in his navy-blue wool robe, and he hugs me to his chest. It's a secret. He's not supposed to be with me or leave his hospital room. He leans down with his big lips and kisses me on the side of my face, deep and warm. A nurse nun comes up the stairs. We freeze and back away. The white-dressed nun smiles and nods pretending that she doesn't know about Dad, and how he is away from his room late, past visiting hours. The nurse nun slips through the door, the rosary beads suspended on her habit clacking as she disappears into the hallway. Mama and Dad huddle in whispers, and I go back to the window to hide my tears. The lights down in the dark valley below blur and become brighter.

We are walking, walking, walking. It's just Mama and me, alone. We must keep going.

V. Layers: Hidden and Broken

Like breathing on glass, an enraptured artist friend once told me, brushing his hand through the air. He was speaking of George Inness's technique of putting color glazes onto canvas. A delicate process, a gradual, translucent layering, creating a mist of color.

How unlike these color layers of glaze are from the geologic layers of anthracite coal in the Lackawanna Valley. The almost pure carbon carries ancient sunlight and fossil plants in the form of opaque mineral blackness.

♦ ♦ ♦

When geologists talk about layers of rock, they use the word *strata*. They use beautiful diagrams to portray the stories of geologic events in a location. Pictured in the diagrams are brick patterns for limestone, or flecks for sandstone, or solid black for coal. Though the stripes of different kinds of rock look neat and clear in a diagram, the illustration represents breaks in geologic patterns separated by millions of years. The boundaries between layers, unconformities, suggest great catastrophes and change—a *loss* of something. Huge events recorded in stone are gone.

Many layers of history and story have been deposited and

removed in the Lackawanna Valley since George Inness painted, beginning with the mining of coal veins, leading to wealth, and then to abandonment. All at once, the life we knew in the Lackawanna Valley and in neighboring coal-mining valleys disappeared. Like a vapor, like the smoke that rose from our land, our greatness slipped away. We lost our identity and importance. Our language and our ideas were frozen in the nineteenth century, and we were left behind. Bypassed. The coal was played out and our nation chose other forms of energy. The long, slow decline of anthracite's dominance began as petroleum, a fossil-fuel cousin, rose as an alternate fuel resource, and our nation transitioned to the freedom of automobiles. Passenger rail disappeared. Mountains and valleys were reshaped as an interstate highway blasted through.

Yet the highway is a thread back to the progress heralded in the Inness painting. The velocity achieved from fossil fuel extraction.

♦ ♦ ♦

Like a geologist, I seek meaning in the deposits of time. I continue to wonder: of those of us who called the Lackawanna Valley home, who were we on the landscape? In history's reckoning, were we mighty and important? Were we "backward," as others called us, because we stayed for our families' sakes and held onto traditions? Or were we simply forgotten and decrepit?

What can help us interpret the sequence of events as our city slowly decayed, as its reasons for being, for existing in that location, disappeared?

—

Memories of coal country are like diagrams of bedrock geology. Between the layers, there is a shift in terrain: a break in time. The memory-holder is, in a way, like coal: carrying the stories of past landscape.

Superimposed upon the living landscape—where decay has continued to take down what is left of breaker buildings and tipples, where rust has hidden rails, and ties have crumbled into creosoted soil—is my childhood's memory landscape. A time and place when so many more people lived and worked in the valley, when visible particulate-filled smoke was the signature of progress, and Scranton's downtown was tall and dark. Sometimes the memory brings newly paved highways, final runs of last trains and crumbling stations, sunlight on dark pavement when the smoke ended, the diminished skyline of my city as buildings burned, leaving gaps or shorter structures. In deeper layers, my memory holds saturated colors: pale blue glass mason jars filled with tomatoes, black diamonds glittering under full sun in passing coal cars, cobalt blue flames at night.

Memory holders are refugees. We are all refugees who left something behind and can't go back to what was. Even if the geographic place we left is still there and intact, our relationship to it has been forever altered.

BRIDGE OF TIME,
RIVER OF PAVEMENT

A change comes over our neighborhood. The coal trains get shorter. Families who live just above the hollow are moved out—their houses are put on great, big trailer trucks and moved to other locations. Where once trees covered the foot of the mountain, and houses of people we knew were scattered in the woods, a great path of destruction, of blasting, takes over. Some houses are knocked down. Large machinery takes away the trees right above the hollow, begins tearing up the earth, and tumbling rocks. It exposes the red ash tailings from the steel mills, dumped into the long-ago ravine that made up our hollow before it became a neighborhood—the ash that our houses are built on. Immense chunks of rocks create a great talus slope above the baseball field and playground at the bottom of our hill. Throughout a whole year of laundry, groceries, church, the machinery blasts and grinds.

A highway is built. It is a bridge from our little place to someplace far away that we know nothing about—a bridge that tries to remove us from the world powered by trains and coal toward a world of automobiles and oil. It separates us from our relatives up on the mountain. Our neighborhood, our little hollow, is no longer intact—it no longer belongs to us. As much as we feel spied upon by the trains, they have been part of our landscape. But the highway neither brings us anything nor takes anything away to the world outside our valley. The interstate highway helps people from elsewhere to pass through as if we who live beside it don't exist.

Skating

"Oh, I loved skating!" Mama says with a big smile.

I sit in my pedal pushers between her and Dad, on the bottom step of the front porch. Dad fits the metal key to the plate of the roller-skate, adjusting the size to fit the lip of my leather-soled shoes. Dad looks happy as he fusses with the key. He tightens it and motions me to the level sidewalk landing.

"Come over here," Dad says. "Try standing."

I shuffle away from the steps, and I try to cross the cement landing leading to the steeply sloping boulevard sidewalk. Because our yard and house are terraced into the hillside, the uphill side of the landing on the left has a waist-high cinder cement wall, and the downhill side on the right has a drop-off to the neighbor's landing. There really isn't much that's level.

I push, I wobble forward, and as Dad shouts "Hang on!" I fling my left hand onto the wall for support, but down I go. Using the wall, I pull myself back up, and keeping my hand along the wall, I can slow and stop. Ahead of me is the boulevard sidewalk, which tilts steeply all the way down our street to the bottom of the hollow. I reach the edge of the landing, put both my hands on the wall, turn, and use my right hand for support to skate the short length back. I push, roll, and bump my knees into the porch steps. I turn and again push my feet and stop with my hands. Start and stop and start again.

All at once the skates spin out from under me and I go down with a bump on rough, cindery concrete. Tears burn in my eyes. "Skating is hard!"

"Skating is fun," Mama encourages.

"Mama, you grew up on a level sidewalk."

With a smile, Mama shakes her head. "You're just trying the skates out here. Later we'll go somewhere where you can go a-ways."

"Come on," Dad says. He reaches beneath my arms and pulls me upright.

I push across the landing. This time I zoom out over the angled sidewalk and feel as if I am flying. I land in the grass boulevard on my knees. After I catch my breath, I crawl back across the steeply angled sidewalk to the landing.

Dad looks at me. "I wonder what would happen if you got onto that sidewalk and started downhill."

"I wouldn't be able to stop!"

"Probably not." Dad smiles. "Maybe you'd keep going to the lower alley—or all the way down to the creek. And then," Dad pauses for emphasis, "you might just start uphill to the mountain if you got a good enough start. Should I give you a push?"

"Dad! No!"

"Just teasing," says Dad. "Okay. The skates fit. You can take them off now."

"Take them off?"

"We're going to go for a ride. Up to the highway," he answers.

"Why?"

"To take a look."

"On the highway? It's open?"

"No. Not yet. But the section up here is paved and ready." Dad points to the huge slope covered in broken boulders across from our hill. "Come on. Let's take a ride and go see."

Dad drives us to the street that leads up to the mountain road. Where rusty red iron ash made our road to the mountain, there's now a bridge, and beneath the bridge are four lanes of paved highway. Though sawhorses signal that the highway is still closed, Dad manages to drive around them, down a small hill, and onto the large, new asphalt road. A double-wide lane stretches as far as we can see in either direction. Above us, towards the railroad tracks and the mountain, there is yet another wide band of asphalt. Dad drives slowly. Looking to our right, we see we are above our hollow.

I am all at once surprised, excited, and delighted. Somehow—if my dad, a firefighter, someone who marches in parades in uniform—somehow, if he thinks it's okay to drive on this piece of new highway, it's got to be okay.

As we look down the new highway, we see a strange open view. All the woods we used to know are gone.

It takes us a moment to orient ourselves…our neighborhood…the hollow…

"Oh look…there's our house!" we shout.

"We could almost shout to ourselves if we were on the front porch," says Dad.

We can see the neighbor's pear and pecan trees that grow just downhill from our house, and we can see the houses at the bottom of the hollow, across from where we are…but the way down there now is impossible—it's blocked by a guardrail, a steep slope of boulders, and a wire fence taller than any of us—cutting us off from the baseball field and creek at the base of our hill.

Above the highway, we can still see the railroad tracks paralleling us. We're so high we can pretend to be a railroad engineer like Uncle Bill. Suddenly I wish we could blow the horn and wave the way he does to someone, anyone in the hollow—but I don't say anything about it to Dad. He's very quiet. By the way he's driving, he doesn't want to attract any attention. Slowly, furtively, Dad continues down the new road.

We look down at all the houses on the hillside of the tree-named streets, houses so close together that their porches compete for the view down to the bottom of the hollow. Alder, Willow, Birch, Beech, Maple—*our* tree streets!

"Look!" Mama says, "there's Grandma's house—and the factory—and look! Cungie's store."

After we pass the last of the tree streets that used to connect us to the mountain, Dad stops the car and sets the parking brake, though there is no hill here to pull the car downward. "Okay," he says to me, "let's get out those skates."

I look at Dad and cannot speak. I'm not sure if he's teasing. When I look to Mama, she just smiles and nods.

"Skate on the highway?"

"Yeah. Do you want to? It's nice and level…"

I am too surprised to answer.

Dad comes around to the back door of the car. "Stick your feet out."

I swing my feet out the open door and Dad snaps the skates onto my shoes. He tightens the key and buckles the straps. I wait until Mama comes around to me. She and Dad set me on my feet, on the most level road I have ever seen.

With Dad on my left, and Mama on my right (just like their places in the front of the car) we start moving, slowly at first, but my wheels try to get ahead of them. Their pace quickens and I am rolling and rattling, flying through the air. My feet are no longer feet. My feet are wings. Mama and Dad begin to run, their leather-soled shoes slapping the pavement.

They run; I fly. *Wheeeee!* we all say, laughing and panting. Out of breath, they slow their steps and brace me for a stop.

"More!" I shout.

"Okay. But give us a chance to breathe." Dad's breathing is shallow, and he is red-faced. It's hard for him, but he likes this, too.

Dad lights a cigarette. Mama takes my hand and pulls

me into motion, slower now, and I push and glide and push and glide holding her good arm, the one that isn't twisted.

When Dad catches up to us, we all reach a new surface. Both he and Mama hold on to me, rolling me onto rough, white concrete, bordered with horizontal metal bars. It's a very high bridge that I've never seen before, and there's something strange about it.

"Mama, there's no sidewalk on this bridge."

"No," Dad answers. "People aren't supposed to walk it. It's for cars."

"Are there waterfalls?"

"Down there? No," Dad laughs softly. "Come look."

Dad holds me as Mama and I peer down between the metal bars to see the bend in the brook—the railroad tracks—the cemetery. We are looking down on our relatives' graves at the edge of our hollow. From up here the cemetery looks sweet—a lawn amid all the dripping green of the beech forest, its tiny white and gray rectangles set against a green carpet. The bridge spans the bend of the waters at the cemetery and crosses away and out of our hollow through an opening that's never existed on this landscape before.

For the return trip we drive back the way we came. Dad seems to be worn out. I look out the window of our car as it creeps along. I see that there's something strange about the road. In some way it's not part of our neighborhood, even though it runs right through it.

"Dad," I try to find a way to ask, "Why don't the streets come up here?"

"Up to the highway, you mean?"

"Why can't we get up here from the streets…drive up here with a car from down there?"

"That's the way it's made. You can't go on and off at each block."

"But why not?"

"It's made so people can pass through quickly. They don't want to stop here." Dad shrugs. "They're going to big cities farther away."

"Then why is the highway *here*?"

"Well, we had no choice about that. It's where the government put it—right through our hollow."

The year slips into fall, then cold, rainy November and Thanksgiving. Dad has the evening paper and it's almost gray dark. He looks up from the paper with an odd smile on his face, then surprises Mama and me with, "Come on, we're going for a ride."

Dad turns the car downhill, but at the bottom, instead of driving down through the hollow, he turns it around and comes back up our hill. He brings us to the street that leads to the mountain road, but instead of crossing the bridge that leads to the mountain, he turns the car down the small, slanted ramp that leads to the interstate highway.

"It's open now." Dad drives downward, but increases speed, faster and faster and faster—and we've never gone this fast before. Not on any road. And he drives faster. He points to a sign. "Sixty-five miles per hour," he tells Mama, who has shrunk back into her seat. The hollow swings past us in a blur, so fast—I cannot see anything I care about.

We whirl through space, through the hollow, past Grandma's house and Cungie's store, over the new bridge, over the cemetery. I hold on to the back of Dad's car seat, and my head is spinning.

Dad slows, goes up a ramp, over a bridge, and turns around and comes back on one of the two lanes next to where we've just gone. Once again, we see our hollow, our houses on the hill, the lopsided back porches perched on poles, and the lines of rope holding laundry.

"This is how people are going to travel now. No more highways through town, or downtown. No more roads along the rivers and tracks. Fast and straight. Right up over the mountains and away." He pauses, "Yep. All this place will be someday is highways."

It isn't the first time Dad has said those words—all this place will be someday is highways…it's a strange thing to say. It rings in my head. What can he mean by that? Does he mean that the houses would disappear? That the coal will run out? Does he mean to say that we won't be here anymore?

I didn't like riding on the highway. Skating on it was so much better—especially with Mama and Dad on either side of me. We were together flying through space, sharing the whole world. Riding on the new interstate highway, the speed we were traveling was too fast. My whole world went by in the blink of an eye.

◆ ◆ ◆

A lifetime goes by in the blink of an eye. But the eye is

blinking, twitching, as the brain struggles, pulsing with stroke. It pulses and goes blank, relieved of any memory, relieved of any duty to any nerve or desire of muscle. It goes blank, and it is done.

Endings

Childhood ended for me when I was eight years old and Dad died.

I had been brushing his thinning hair. It was a game we played—I brushed his balding head to make his hair grow, as Mama said brushing would do—and he teased me and made faces pretending he was a small child. I sat above him in the dark green armchair. All at once, Dad got up, wheezing, walking between rooms. We were used to his troubled breathing and troubled heart, but this was strange.

I heard him say his last words in a desperate tone, "I feel dizzy. I have to sit down."

He groped his way from the kitchen to the middle room and, finding the green armchair, fell heavily into it. His breathing quickened, his mouth opened, and he began to shake. His eyes rolled back. His legs and arms stiffened while he panted. It seemed to go on for a very long time.

"Dad! Daddy!" I cried. An asthma attack? A heart attack? Mama stayed in the kitchen and stared out the back door—no words, no movement.

His stubbly face reddened as if he were strangling. *Asthma*, I thought. *Water! He needs water!* With my hands shaking, I ran to the kitchen and grabbed a glass, filled it, and returned to the chair.

"Dad!" I called to him, panicked. "Drink water to be okay, okay?" I patted his face, put the glass to his lips. Though I managed to get his lips parted, his tongue was curled upward, stuck to his palate. I pried his mouth open and poured the water in. Water dribbled over his chin and black t-shirt, as he shook and rocked. Through his half-open eyelids, only the whites of his eyes showed.

I wanted to find some comfort for him or me.

"I'll brush your hair, okay?" I climbed above him on the flat chair back with the brush in my hand and gently pulled across his head.

Dad gave no response. The shaking lessened, though.

Tears rolled down his cheeks. All year it had been heart attacks and hemorrhages. Ropes, my relatives told me, were put up his nose and down his throat, to stop the bleeding. Ambulances. Calls from the fire station that he had collapsed on the job.

Mama stood in the kitchen, staring out the door with her left hand across her middle and right hand cradling chin and cheek. She didn't speak, but shook. Tears fell.

I didn't know what was happening to her or Dad. I couldn't do anything to make Dad talk. I didn't know then that the stroke took speech away, that it took his whole mind away that day, in those few minutes. I didn't know what to do but to go outdoors onto the cinder-cement wall. I stood with my hands at my side, crying.

I didn't hear the neighbor calling my name until she was beside me, looking concerned.

"It's my dad," I sobbed.

She took the information and called the ambulance.

Men in white uniforms arrived. I was back at Dad's side, telling him what was happening. The ambulance crew—men familiar to me from the fire station, coworkers of my dad—came into the room with the metal stretcher. I told them how I tried to give my dad water, but I couldn't get him to answer me, that maybe it was an asthma attack. They nodded and loaded him onto the metal stretcher, struggling with his big weight, struggling, to carry him down the steep steps to the awaiting ambulance.

I never saw him alive after that.

I heard about what happened in the hospital the next day, when Mama told the relatives who arrived.

"It was peaceful-like, you know? The color came back into his face, and he looked *so* beautiful. Then the nurse came in and said he was gone," Mama said, amazed, her mouth twisted up in a bemused smile. She didn't cry about it. Never after did she show grief. "They said it was—a what-do-you-call-it?—a cerebral hemorrhage, a brain hemorrhage. And they said if he had lived, he would have been a 'vegetable.' His brain was all gone-like, you know?"

The next day, it was clear that a journey had begun for Mama and me. For a long time, I rocked in a chair in silence, looking at the beige paint on the living room wall.

Relations began arriving, holding me and letting me run outdoors and back in as I needed to. Women's voices swirled around us.

"God called him home."

"He's in heaven now, with Jesus."

"He won't suffer anymore."

"He's in a good place."

"It was his time."

I saw Dad only one more time, as a blue-lipped corpse in a coffin. He had on a beautiful, full pinstripe suit, and his shoes were highly polished. His hair was slicked back, thin as ever. I tried to look at him, this dead man, and pray the way I was taught to do over so many bodies in coffins, but all I could do was search his face, looking for peace. Grandma arrived, wailing loudly, and rushed forward. Someone ushered me away and took me to a relative's house somewhere closer to the cemetery and brook.

On the day of the funeral, we were driven in a procession to the cemetery, crossing all the streets back to the brook—River, Hickory, Alder, Willow, Birch, Beech, Maple, Elm, Locust, Cherry...and finally over the plank bridge into the edge of the hollow where the cemetery lay.

Though Dad didn't die in a fire, the Brotherhood of Firefighters was there to bear his casket, six of them. That was the hardest scene for all of us—the uniformed men, his coworkers, their faces tight and sad, bearing the flag-draped casket.

It was a strange scene at the cemetery—not because we had brought yet another member of the family to this place, but because of the presence of the new highway bridge looming above us. The gray cement and metal bridge was blank-looking—faceless, it seemed out of place in scale and design with the brook and headstone-dotted landscape. We could no longer hear the shushing waters, or trains. Instead, we heard a ceaseless whooshing, but could not see any car, or train, or person. It crossed high above us, that highway, and no one in any of the cars or trucks speeding over that bridge knew we were there in our landscape of grief.

All that was left of my father went to the cellar: a scratchy, navy blue wool uniform sweater, and the black fireman's rubber boots. The metal snap buckles on the boots were shaped like little black ladders—like fire escapes left suspended on the sides of brick buildings and alleyways, so much more noticeable after a building had burned and collapsed. Metal stairways that never quite touched the ground.

◆ ◆ ◆

The image I was left with for many years was of the green armchair: dark green, broad and flat, whose textured surface lay in swirling patches. The chair in which Dad had begun his journey away from us. As if it were a world, a landscape I could get lost in, I ran my fingers over the chair's softly nubby surface, the texture of rivers carving valleys, with islands of trees—no rails, or roads, or people. A landscape shaped of the forested wildness that our land had once been, with deep and sinuous curves of valleys.

Some Other City

In the 1960s and 1970s, the Lackawanna Valley continued to crumble. Though interstate highways had reached
us, those of us still dwelling in the valley never truly left
the nineteenth century in our way of thinking. It would be
years before I read Adlai Stevenson's words about my city
being a hellhole, but the grim realities, along with the put-
downs, were everywhere. Fires raged beneath our city, and
culm dumps burned day and night, as if we were already
eternally damned, no matter which religion we believed.
No matter what we did. While parts of our city fell into the
mines, we continued our longing for coal and rails to save
us. It's who we *were.*

Teachers planted in me the seeds of wanting to see
Europe and Asia, to sail away over the mountains. Meanwhile, relatives and neighbors kept my feet on the ground,
down in the valley, reminding me endlessly that this is
where I belonged. Grown and needing more in life than
desperation, I made the choice to leave.

But how to cross over from one century to the next?

I did it by riding a train to a beautiful Midwestern university town. Beyond the blue edge of my childhood imag-

inings, I crossed over the mountains and didn't look back. I was no longer left behind by a string of railcars passing. I was, instead, a passenger on a train leaving Pennsylvania's mountains. Through the train window, the view presented one snowy mountain after another as we rode into the night. We swung from one side of a valley to the other, pushing through tunnels, hugging mountains above streetlights and homes of valley people in nameless towns until, in the darkness, we swept around one curve so large, we could see both the engine lights and parlor car from the middle coach.

At dawn, the world flattened. We traversed a huge soil blanket with only a few wrinkles, which smoothed as we traveled west. Trees diminished, becoming farther apart and more stunted. The snow blinded us with whiteness. Fewer trees. Fewer shadows. Less hidden. *Less to hide*, I thought.

My new home took my breath away. The university town was everything I could have dreamed of: liveliness, whole and occupied downtown buildings, restaurants and stores open at night, people walking the streets, buses, and bicycles—commerce. Buildings had windows, whole and clean, filled with clothes and art. Everywhere, people filled the sidewalks, shopping, talking, laughing, reading. What struck me most were the faces of the others my age, with clear, perfect skin and pearly white smiles of straight teeth.

At first, the excitement of settling into my new home took my attention away from one detail: an odor. There was a familiar, dark odor coming from the edge of campus, where silver steel rails cut across the street intersection at an odd angle: railroad tracks. I had to follow them.

As I turned the corner, my heart fell. The odor was all too familiar. Coal. Peaked piles of coal mounded at the campus power plant, dumped from an elevator, appearing for all the world as miniature culm dumps without the flames. Coal to fuel the electricity for the university. It sat fenced-in behind chain-link—except for the coal that had spilled out from beneath and rattled across the sidewalk at my feet. Pieces of black diamonds scattered across the cement walk, staining it rust red. I had come so far from coal country and still couldn't leave its stain behind. Above me, immense coal furnaces rumbled and clattered, vibrating the air. I looked up. A shiver coursed through my body.

There, on a sidetrack next to the campus power plant, were the rusting black gondola cars bearing the name of my valley in fading white letters: *Lackawanna*.

VI. In Pigment: Seeing the Light

I left the Lackawanna Valley with the intention of never returning. Over time and across distance, I carried little of my childhood in coal country and had forgotten about the Inness painting until I saw a print of *The Lackawanna Valley* in the form of a copy-paper-sized reproduction. By that time, I was working in a science museum in St. Paul. The print hung on the outside wall of my co-worker's cubicle. It caught me: *The Lackawanna Valley*. Familiar. Engaging. Beautiful. Frightening. Each time I went to consult with Tom on our exhibit, I paused before it, searching. I searched it for meaning, for answers, and still wondered where that boy with the straw hat lay on the landscape long ago, where George Inness had stood. *He must have been halfway downslope from the hill where I stood as a little girl, looking westward over the valley.* Yet something didn't seem right. Something about the locomotive. From my side of the valley, the locomotive should have headed to the right instead of bearing left. The tracks must have been re-routed. Or so I thought.

As I stood there lost in a small print of a nineteenth-century landscape painting, Tom came up beside me. "You know that painting?" he asked. *"The Lackawanna Valley?"*

I hesitated. "Yep. I grew up there. In that valley, I

mean." I didn't really want to connect myself to the Lackawanna Valley, the place that had gained a reputation for
collapse, ignorance, desolation, and illegal trades. But I
told Tom about the trains, coal, culm dumps, glorious sunsets, and endless mountains. I also told him how I puzzled
over the view and wondered where the boy in the painting
lay.

"I hope to see it for real one day." I pointed to the print.
"National Gallery in D. C., right?"

"Um hmm." Tom nodded. "Do you want this copy? I
can get another."

And then what he said stunned me. "You know there's
an Inness exhibit in town, right? At the Art Institute. It will
still be there this weekend. That painting is there."

"You're kidding."

"No!" Tom laughed. "Go check it out!"

The Inness painting was huge, the scale of it making me
feel small, its colors softer and more amber-toned than any
reproductions I had seen. I stood before *The Lackawanna
Valley* searching for answers in the swirls of paint on canvas—and I found the answer I had sought all those years.
All the reproductions of the painting caught the details so
well: the locomotive, the roundhouse, the boy, the many
layers of greenery, the mountains, immutable, in the background, and the vast sky. But now I saw what I had missed
all along: the iron furnaces sending two distinct streams of
smoke straight upward, like a ghostly set of parallel rails
knitting land and sky together. The iron furnaces that made
the rails and gave birth to the city of Scranton—the ones

whose remains were on my side of the valley—were in the center background of the painting, sending columns of smoke that made that glorious haze.

My eyes drifted upward in the painting. Something about the mountain edges in the background seemed wrong. I looked closer and caught my breath. They weren't the West Mountains after all. There in the distance was the familiar gap at the edge of East Mountain, the source of the Stafford-Meadow Brook that made its way, shushing, past the cemetery where all my relatives lay—the beginning of my hollow. Now I understood: the boy was not looking *westward* across the valley from my side at dusk. The boy in the painting was gazing *eastward*, at morning time. The view in the painting was of a rosy dawn heralding new beginnings.

The boy was gazing eastward at dawn, and I was looking back over his shoulder to the Lackawanna Valley from west of the river and mountains.

THE *WORLD BOOK* SPEAKS

World Book Encyclopedia 1971, volume 17, S page 188:

Scranton

SCRANTON, Pa. (pop. 111, 443; met. Area 234, 531; alt. 725 ft.), is the largest city in Pennsylvania's anthracite region, and one of the largest cities in the state. **At one time, the economy of the Scranton region depended solely on coal. But mining has declined,** and Scranton has become a major center for manufacture of textiles, household appliances, shoes, cigars, and electronic equipment. Its name comes from the Scranton family, which founded an ironworks there in 1840.

Scranton lies in northeastern Pennsylvania, 134 miles from New York City. The city stands in a deep valley closely bordered by ridges of the Allegheny Mountains. It is a short distance from the Pocono Mountains resort area. For location, see PENNSYLVANIA (political map).

Scranton is the home of the International Correspondence Schools. Also located in Scranton are the University of Scranton, Marywood College, and a Pennsylvania State University extension school.

Scranton has a large wholesale and retail trade. Besides coal, the city produces heating and air conditioning equipment, textile machinery, has tabs, caskets stokers, plastic products, and paints and varnishes. Other products include books, clothing, lamps, condensers, paper boxes, and phonograph records.

The first settlers came in the 1780's. Scranton became a borough in 1853, and a city in 1866. It has a mayor-council form of government.   S.K. Stevens

VII. Through the Lens: Sunrise View

In May 2003, National Park Ranger Ken Ganz, of Steamtown National Historic Site, knocked on the door of an apartment building in Scranton, Pennsylvania. This building, located on the west bank of the Lackawanna River, would give him the view he wanted. The knock on the door awoke the building's owner. Ken asked if he could climb to the top of the building. Permission granted, Ken then ascended four flights carrying his camera and a postcard-sized copy of George Inness's *The Lackawanna Valley*. The ranger knew he had the perfect day.

Ken was on a quest to find the spot where Inness had stood as he composed his landscape. Visitors intrigued with the famous Inness painting often asked him about the vantage point. For Ken, this quest was also a personal one. Ken's love of railroads, art, and American history had brought him back to the Lackawanna Valley, where he had been born, to tell its story. He remembered seeing Inness's painting when he was a child and had, like many, wondered if he could find that spot.

The ranger looked out from the building's roof onto Lackawanna Avenue, and then over to Bridge 60, an iron railroad bridge crossing the Lackawanna River. The rails, formerly Delaware, Lackawanna, and Western, belonged now to the most recent company that absorbed all the rail lines in the area and ran a hodge-podge of locomotives. With the postcard in hand, Ken peered through the camera's viewfinder. He told me of that moment: "I felt a chill down my spine. Lackawanna Avenue through the lens lined up perfectly with the painting's depiction of it." The memories of seeing the Inness painting in his childhood came flooding back. He could hear his parents' voices telling him, "This is who we are—this is where we come from."

At nine-thirty in the morning, the sun was rising over the eastern edge of the mountains, laying out for Ken Ganz the landscape George Inness had painted. Ken began taking pictures. His telephoto lens foreshortened the view and distance to line up exactly with what Inness had depicted in oils. The light was that of early summer, in the morning time, and a train was crossing the bridge over the tree-lined Lackawanna River.

Satisfied with the photos, Ken solicited a Park Service artist's help to produce a combined image that contrasted 150 years.

I was unprepared for the landscape images Ken photographed and sent to me via computer, showing what remained of the city's downtown. I looked at the images of the Scranton I had known. All the tall downtown buildings I knew were gone, erased from the scene, as were the trestles and railyards. Nearly fifty years had passed since I had been a child in that place, and it was now unrecognizable to me. I had grown up in another century, raised on the images and cultural vestiges of the century that preceded me. The landscape continued to change in its peculiar pattern of progress. All that is familiar to me in a twenty-first-century scene are the mountain edges.

Afterword

On our planet Earth we are interdependent, connected across the world to places and people we may never see. Though *Black Diamonds: A Childhood Colored by Coal* is a personal geography, the story connects humanity's choices around the globe. I wrote it to honor a people and history I felt had become lost, and I wrote it as a way of understanding the choices before us.

When I was growing up, the world seemed large, dark, and mysterious. Perhaps that's true for many children, but I grew up in a coal-strewn landscape of ghosts of greatness—abandoned rails and roads; large nineteenth-century city buildings mostly empty on the upper floors, their blank windows staring out like sad, dark eyes of old men; burned-out buildings, their ornate exteriors deformed along with their twisted steel skeletons; boarded sidewalks keeping us separated from the remains of the most recent fires. The land was ashen while the skies were gray-white with smoke and turned to darkness when fog rolled in.

We children of the Lackawanna Valley in the 1960s lived in confusion. We were raised to be fiercely proud of our land and our place in history, but we felt the helplessness of our elders. What we saw on television—possibilities and choices, colorful consumerism—didn't match our reality. It was as if we lived on a completely different planet. We grew up witnessing downtown buildings implode along with the bridges we knew. And what was erased from the scene was never quite replaced with the same sense of magnificence or hope.

The fossil fuel coal is still used—primarily in the production of electricity—and is the most major contributor to climate change. Coal-fired power plants produce one fifth of all global greenhouse gas emissions—more than any other single source.

I'm aware that life was so very different before the use of coal. I often wonder if I could have lived in a landscape without all the conveniences it provided—light and heat for homes, for example. Having grown up in the land of coal, I always wished for another reality for everyone in my valley and beyond: cleaner and healthier for everyone in the world.

I believe we are now at a different point in history. We must look through the present to future generations for whom we can not only imagine, but create a safe and sustainable world with renewable energy.

Acknowledgments

The name *Lackawanna* is from the Lenape people who are indigenous to present-day Northeastern Pennsylvania. It means "fork in the river," the name given to the place where Roaring Brook meets the Lackawanna River; the place that became the site of the steel mills and rail yards and later, downtown Scranton, Pennsylvania. I wish to acknowledge the Lackawanna Valley as the traditional land of the Lenape people who were pushed away from their home over 200 years ago, and that their ancient culture has been, and continues to be, carried through story interwoven with land.

So many people gave support to *Black Diamonds* over the quarter-century since its beginnings: my mentor, the late writer, Ben Logan, whose thoughtful portrait of place, *The Land Remembers* sings in my heart, and who was willing to share his writing knowledge with this fledgling writer; Marshall Cook, creative writing instructor, who generously encouraged the writing as I began putting story on paper all the way through to my MFA program; the support of Deborah Buffton and Lila Marmel, who assisted in times of overwhelming disability.

I send my gratitude to the Terry Foundation and the wonderful people at Edenfred and Write On Door County for their support through residencies.

Thoughtful readers gave their input: Dr. Walt Jacobs, Ken Whiteash, Gretchen Boeren, Tami Dettinger, Tanace Matthiesen, and Sue Presser. I am eternally grateful to the people of the University of British Columbia's Optres MFA program: Andrew Gray, Annabel Lyon, Wayne Grady, Merilyn Simonds, and my classmates around the globe, for a powerful, international, accessible learning experience. Special recognition goes to writer, classmate, and friend, Tara Gilboy, for support and encouragement.

Artists Alvin Felch, David Wells, and Diana Randolph expanded my sense of George Inness's work by helping me see how his landscape painting is crafted to lead the viewer on a journey. For me, the journey continues.

This project received the support of a lifelong friend, Reverend William G. Buffton, whose insights as a former miner within Scranton's Welsh-American community contributed to my understanding of the lives and work of miners and breaker boys going back to the late nineteenth century.

I celebrate Mr. Frank Cicci, teacher and storyteller extraordinaire who, through his hard work, wished for his students to become good citizens. (I hope I fulfill that role.) Likewise, I celebrate the public school teachers in my place of origin who long ago fought for dignity. And I wish to honor my father, Ben, a storyteller and Scranton firefighter, who, along with the Brotherhood of Firefighters then and now, keep us safe.

I send a special thank you to R. R. Young, who added finishing touches, a dab here or there, giving depth to my own portrait of the Lackawanna Valley.

Having worked as a cultural interpreter for the National Park Service, I know the dedication of NPS employees to preserving our heritage, and often individual rangers do not receive the recognition they deserve. I recognize Kenny Ganz of Steamtown National Historic site for sharing his exquisite knowledge and love of the history of American railroads, Scranton, and George Inness's painting *The Lackawanna Valley*.

To everyone from my childhood in the Lackawanna Valley whose stories have graced my life and who have given me the opportunity to send our stories forward as an essential piece of American history, I send thanks. Stories last longer than a relationship, or a substance. Story is all we are left with when someone passes; all we leave behind when we go, is story. So, for those who share bloodlines with me—I honor all we lived through with this story.

My gratitude goes to everyone at Torrey House Press for the care and kindness they have given *Black Diamonds*. I deeply connect with and share their concern for social and environmental justice, and I feel honored by their work.

Most of all, I am grateful to the children I raised, Leif and Celeste, whose curiosity about where I come from and whose love of story began the journey of this book.

About the Author

Catherine Young worked as a national park ranger, farmer, educator, and mother before putting her heart into her writing. She earned her MFA in Creative Writing at the University of British Columbia, and holds degrees in Geography, Environmental Science, and Education. Catherine is author of the ecopoetry collection *Geosmin* and her prose and poetry is published nationally and internationally. She deeply believes in the use of story and art as tools for transforming the world, and she holds concern for water. Rooted in farm life, Catherine writes with a keen sense of place and lives with her family in the ancient unglaciated Driftless Area of Wisconsin.

Find podcasts and more at
www.catherineyoungwriter.com.

About Torrey House Press

Torrey House Press exists at the intersection of the literary arts and environmental advocacy. THP publishes books that elevate diverse perspectives, explore relationships with place, and deepen our connections to the natural world and to each other. THP inspires ideas, conversation, and action on issues that link the American West to the past, present, and future of the ever-changing Earth.

Visit www.torreyhouse.org for reading group discussion guides, author interviews, and more.

As a 501(c)(3) nonprofit publisher, our work is made possible by generous donations from readers like you.

Join the Torrey House Press family and give today at www.torreyhouse.org/give.

Torrey House Press is supported by the King's English Bookshop, Maria's Bookshop, the Jeffrey S. & Helen H. Cardon Foundation, the Sam & Diane Stewart Family Foundation, the Literary Arts Emergency Fund, the Mellon Foundation, the Barker Foundation, Diana Allison, Klaus Bielefeldt, Joe Breddan, Karen Edgley, Laurie Hilyer, Susan Markley, Kitty Swenson, Shelby Tisdale, Kirtly Parker Jones, Robert Aagard & Camille Bailey Aagard, Kif Augustine Adams & Stirling Adams, Rose Chilcoat & Mark Franklin, Jerome Cooney & Laura Storjohann, Linc Cornell & Lois Cornell, Susan Cushman & Charlie Quimby, Kathleen Metcalf & Peter Metcalf, Betsy Gaines Quammen & David Quammen, the Utah Division of Arts & Museums, Utah Humanities, the National Endowment for the Humanities, the Salt Lake City Arts Council, the Utah Governor's Office of Economic Development, and Salt Lake County Zoo, Arts & Parks. Our thanks to our readers, donors, members, and the Torrey House Press Board of Directors for their valued support.